Additional praise for *Performance Cycling*

*Dave has been coaching, racing, and riding for years,
and really knows the ins and outs on why
the body works the way it does.*

—Alison Dunlap, 2001 Mountain Bike World
Champion, 2-time Olympian

Performance **cycling**

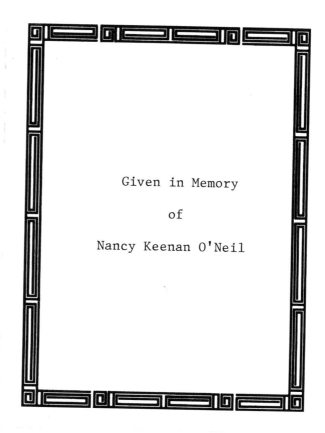

Performance cycling

Training for Power, Endurance, and Speed

David Morris

Ragged Mountain Press / McGraw-Hill

Camden, Maine • New York • Chicago • San Francisco • Lisbon • London • Madrid • Mexico City • Milan • New Delhi • San Juan • Seoul • Singapore • Sydney • Toronto

The McGraw·Hill Companies

2 3 4 5 6 7 8 9 0 DOC DOC 0 10 9 8 7 6 5 4 3

Copyright © 2003 by David Morris

Library of Congress Cataloging-in-Publication Data
Morris, David, 1966 June 9–
  Performance cycling : training for power, endurance, and speed / David Morris.
    p.   cm.
  Includes bibliographical references and index.
  ISBN 0-07-141091-0
  1. Cycling—Training. I. Title.
  GV1048.M67 2003
  796.6—dc21   2003002516

Questions regarding the content of this book should be addressed to
Ragged Mountain Press
P.O. Box 220
Camden, ME 04843
www.raggedmountainpress.com

Questions regarding the ordering of this book should be addressed to
The McGraw-Hill Companies
Customer Service Department
P.O. Box 547
Blacklick, OH 43004
Retail customers: 1-800-262-4729
Bookstores: 1-800-722-4726

Photographs and illustrations by the author.

Contents

Part Three: Training Aids

Acknowledgments

I would like to express my gratitude to two members of the physiology staff of the U.S. Olympic Committee, Dr. Randy Wilber and Paige Holm, M.S., R.D., whose careful reviews and insightful comments helped me to improve the quality of this book. I also greatly appreciate the efforts of Alison Dunlap, Mari Holden, Jane Quigley, and Jon Retseck. Their letters of support for this manuscript played a helpful role in bringing it to market. Finally, thanks to D. A. for leading by example—I'll never forget it.

Preface

When I was studying exercise physiology and racing bicycles as an undergraduate at the University of Missouri, I realized that a giant information gap existed between the scientists doing research on human performance and the athletes and coaches this research was designed to benefit. In 1992, after completing my master's degree, I went to work as a sports physiologist at the U.S. Olympic Training Center (USOTC) in Colorado Springs. I devoted much of my time there to testing, educating, and advising cyclists and their coaches. Despite my efforts, I was only able to reach a small percentage of the athletes who could benefit from the existing scientific information. Two years after leaving the USOTC to pursue my doctorate in exercise physiology, I started work as the sports physiologist for the U.S. Cycling Federation's (USCF) Project '96, where I developed the training programs used by Sky Christopherson to win the national kilometer title in 1995 and by Jane Quigley to win a silver medal in the points race at the World Championships in 1996.

Despite the success of the national team athletes I trained, I recognized that relatively few of the contributions made by scientists to the sport of cycling were being presented to cyclists and coaches in a useful manner. Thus, since the Olympic Games in 1996, I have attempted to disseminate such information to the cycling public. Over the past several years I have continued my excercise physiology research and, as a coach, have designed training programs for and consulted with cyclists of varying abilities.

I wrote *Performance Cycling* to provide cyclists with better information about advances in training methods. My years of experience conducting and reviewing research on cycling performance, competing as a road cyclist and mountain biker myself, and coaching cyclists of all abilities enable me to present this information from the combined perspectives of a scientist, athlete, and coach. I think *Performance Cycling* is the most comprehensive and straightforward guide available to making cyclists' bodies as strong as possible.

Introduction: Cycling and Science Come of Age

For over a hundred years, athletes have been participating in organized bicycle racing. Until recently, cyclists and coaches had to learn about training and equipment through trial and error. Only over the past two or three decades has science been applied to help train cyclists, provide them with better nourishment, and improve their equipment. Because of science, today's cyclists drink carbohydrate drinks instead of water; they no longer smoke cigarettes to "open up their lungs"; they ride on stronger, lighter, and more aerodynamic equipment; and they have more efficient and effective training programs at their disposal. The result? Cyclists are riding faster than ever, as evidenced by the rate at which records are being broken.

But science also has provided cyclists with potentially harmful performance-enhancing supplements such as steroids, human growth hormone, and erythropoietin (EPO). Most of these substances were first isolated and then synthetically manufactured as legitimate medical treatments for disease. However, when sports scientists, coaches, and athletes became aware of the potential benefits of these performance-enhancing drugs, a moral dilemma began to take shape. Many athletes and coaches, citing the potential harmful side effects and the ethical considerations, refused to use the new drugs. Others, deciding that the benefits justified the risks and that winning was the only concern, took the drugs and initially benefited from their use. However, in many cases, athletes were disqualified and suffered serious long-term side effects from the use of performance-enhancing drugs.

The ethical dilemma has not been isolated to physiological questions: recently, utilizing wind tunnels, computer analyses, and exotic materials, engineers and biomechanists have designed equipment that is lighter, stronger, and more aerodynamic than any previously seen in the cycling industry. Once again, however, these advancements have come with costs, as the expense of research and development of today's exotic materials has pushed the price of some equipment beyond the reach of many competitors. For this reason (and others known only to the Union Cycliste Internationale), severe restrictions have been placed on many qualities of the modern bicycle that seriously curtail scientific contributions to bicycle design.

Just as the debate over the benefits versus the drawbacks of sports science is sure to continue in the foreseeable future, two other trends are certain—athletes will continue to do what they can to improve themselves and their ability to compete, and sports scientists will continue to search for ways to assist athletes in their pursuit of perfection.

Preparing a cyclist for competition is a multifaceted undertaking that should take into consideration physiology, nutrition, psychology, and the demands of competition. *Performance Cycling* provides cyclists with a comprehensive approach to preparing for competition that is superior to traditional preparation strategies, which don't combine practical experiences and scientific research. This book teaches how to integrate the latest scientific information into the practical issues of training and preparing for competition.

Over the years, I have worked with cyclists from all ability levels, and all of these riders, from novice category 5 racers to world champions, have had one thing in common: the desire to become faster and stronger. Following the training approach presented in this book in no way guarantees that you will win a world championship, as an accomplishment of this magnitude requires a number of ingredients beyond a person's control. However, the program has been meticulously developed through a combination of scientific research and practical applications in the peloton, and following these concepts will help you become a stronger cyclist.

Part One offers information about human anatomy and physiology and places special emphasis on how the body responds to exercise training. Nutritional issues vital to exercise performance are covered in chapter 2, with particular attention placed on the use of carbohydrates, fats, and proteins as energy sources. Chapter 3 discusses procedures designed to evaluate an athlete's ability to perform work, to determine proper training loads, and to monitor responses to exercise training.

Part Two explains how to use the infomation presented in Part One to develop an effective training program. You will learn how to tailor your program to fit your needs throughout the competitive and off-seasons. And if you'd like a little more guidance in developing a training program, chapter 9 offers tips on selecting a qualified coach.

Part Three deals with the use of ergogenic aids. I have put a great deal of effort into this section, and this review of ergogenic aids is, to my knowledge, more in-depth and comprehensive than can be found in any other book of this type. Throughout my career as a cyclist and exercise physiologist, I have seen fellow athletes spend countless dollars on nutritional supplements that claim to improve exercise performance. Much of this money has not been well spent, since the vast majority of supplements are not ergogenic at all and do nothing to improve athletic performance. This section is intended to provide information on many products now on the market and help you objectively evaluate the efficacy of these and future products.

Part One

THE
HUMAN
BODY

The extreme demands of bicycle racing require significant contributions from multiple physiological systems.

CHAPTER 1

Anatomy of the Machine

Several complex, interrelated systems work together to enable a human body to function and survive. Because competitive cycling is so physically demanding, understanding human anatomy and physiology is essential to making smart training and racing decisions. This chapter provides a brief overview of those anatomical and physiological systems essential to the success of a competitive cyclist.

Muscular System

Skeletal muscle is a protein-based tissue that possesses the abilities to contract and relax. These characteristics allow the muscular system to act as the engine that provides the power for movement. Each individual muscle is composed of tiny muscle fibers bundled together into *motor units*. A motor unit consists of muscle fibers and a nerve that innervates the fibers. For a contraction to occur, the central nervous system sends a signal via the nerve of a particular motor unit. Once that signal arrives, the muscle fibers of the motor unit create tension. When enough tension is developed, the muscle shortens, and movement occurs. When groups of muscles work together, complex movements, like pedaling a bicycle, are accomplished.

The number of motor units in a muscle depends on its tasks. For instance, the quadriceps muscles in our thighs possess many motor units composed of relatively large muscle fibers, allowing these muscles to generate large amounts of force. In contrast, the muscles controlling our eyelids have relatively few motor units composed of small muscle fibers, as little force is required to blink an eye.

Energy Supplies

Muscular contractions are fueled by three energy sources—carbohydrates, fats, and proteins. Of these three substrates, carbohydrate is by far the most versatile: it can be burned quickly without oxygen to provide an immediate source of energy, or it can combine with oxygen to provide a more plentiful yet less rapidly available energy supply. In contrast, fats and proteins must combine with oxygen before they can be used as energy. The process of combining oxygen with the three energy substrates takes place in specialized bodies, known as *mitochondria*, within each muscle cell. Mitochondria are often referred to as the "powerhouses" of the cell because it is within these organelles that the majority of the energy used for muscular contractions is liberated. The number and size of the mitochondria can vary considerably from one motor unit to another based on the type of muscle fiber within the unit and how well the muscle fibers of the unit are trained. Exercise training increases the number and size of mitochondria within a muscle fiber, as working muscle requires large amounts of energy to perform its tasks.

Muscle Fiber Types

Though all skeletal muscle is similar in its makeup and function, subtle differences among muscle fibers can significantly affect the performance capabilities of an individual. In the early 1970s, exercise physiologists began studying these differences by using muscle biopsies to remove small samples of muscle tissue from the body. Upon examining these tissue samples, scientists noticed distinct characteristics that allowed them to categorize muscle fibers into groups. When the individual fibers were electrically stimulated, it was observed that the contractile speed of one type of muscle fiber was slower than another, and this led to the categorization of *slow-twitch* and *fast-twitch* muscle fibers. Researchers also noticed that areas surrounding slow-twitch fibers were rich in glycogen (stored carbohydrates) and that slow-twitch fibers contained many mitochondria, making them adept at combining oxygen with carbohydrates, fats, and proteins to provide energy for muscular contractions. These traits make slow-twitch fibers relatively resistant to fatigue, and because of this, slow-twitch fibers are utilized extensively during activities that require low to moderate amounts of strength over long periods of time.

Observations of fast-twitch fibers revealed fewer mitochondria than found in their slow-twitch counterparts. This means that fast-twitch fibers are not very proficient at utilizing oxygen and fatigue quickly. However, an advantage that the fast-twitch fiber holds over its slower-twitching counterpart is the faster speed at which it can contract and the greater amount of force it can produce during a contraction. Thus, fast-twitch fibers are used extensively in short-burst activities like sprinting or jumping, in which explosive force production takes precedence over endurance.

Not long after the discovery of fast- and slow-twitch muscle fibers, a hybrid fiber was distinguished from the two groups. This new fiber type was found to possess the powerful twitch characteristics of a fast-twitch fiber but was able to use oxygen proficiently, which gave it the fatigue resistance of a slow-twitch fiber. Dubbed the *fast-twitch oxidative* (oxygen-using) fiber, it became the third muscle fiber group accepted by the majority of scientists.

Since these early classifications, improved scientific techniques have allowed physiologists to study muscle fibers more precisely than in past years. We can now observe differences in amino acid composition between fast- and slow-twitch fibers (amino acids being the building blocks of muscle protein) and relate those differences to the twitch characteristics. Classification of muscle fibers based on amino acid composition has allowed us to identify many more muscle fiber types than the original three. Indeed, some physiologists now believe there may be dozens of types. Thus, within the scientific community that studies muscle fiber types, fibers are no longer divided into one of three groups but are thought to exist along a continuum ranging from the fastest, most fatigable to the slowest, most fatigue resistant.

Ever since muscle fiber types were first identified, a debate has raged over whether one type can change into another. That is, can a slower-twitch fiber convert into a faster one, and vice versa? The fiber composition of an athlete's muscles has been shown to have a significant effect on his or her success in athletic events. For instance, the fastest sprinters in both running and cycling have been found to possess a higher ratio of faster fibers in their legs than their counterparts who are successful in long-distance events. The question then becomes, "Can we train muscle fibers to convert?" If this were possible, it could lead coaches and athletes to rethink the way they train.

Early work on both animal and human subjects provided no definitive evidence that muscle fibers could change their type. With the recent developments in muscle fiber typing, however, sports scientists have been able to observe definite fiber type changes in rats, cats, dogs, birds, and primates, including humans.

This concept of fiber type transformation is a relatively new development in the field of exercise physiology. I became aware of the research in 1993 while studying under Dr. Steve Alway at Ohio State University. Dr. Alway and his associates were working with novel methods of forcing faster-twitch muscle fibers to perform the work of their slower-twitching counterparts and vice versa. Alway noticed that following several weeks of this manipulation, fiber type changes would occur. These results induced me to reassess the approach I used to train cyclists. As a result, the training programs I now prescribe are quite different from those I used myself when I was racing competitively prior to 1993.

Digestive System

Consumption and processing of food is vital for maintaining body tissues and providing fuel for the enormous number of physiological processes necessary for life. In the mouth, food is chewed and broken down into pieces small enough to swallow. The stomach breaks down food further and passes it into the small intestine, which finishes the process and provides a place for nutrients to be absorbed into the bloodstream. After passing through the small intestine, the remaining food, divested of nearly all its nutrients, enters the large intestine, where much of the water that was mixed with the food during digestion is reabsorbed. The unusable or unneeded compounds that remain pass from the body as waste products.

After being absorbed into the bloodstream, nutrients are transported to the areas of the body where they are most urgently needed or to other tissues for storage. Proteins are taken to muscle and other tissues, where they are used for maintaining structural integrity or repairing damage. Fats and carbohydrates are taken to working muscle or other metabolically active areas and burned for their energy. Supplies of these substrates in excess of current energy demands are stored in the body—carbohydrates in the liver or skeletal muscle as glycogen, and fats in the adipose (fatty) tissue as body fat.

Endocrine System

The endocrine system is composed of several hormone-secreting glands, cells, and groups of cells located throughout the body. *Hormones* are chemical substances that exert specific physiological controls over cells and tissues. For instance, erythropoietin is a hormone secreted by cells within the kidney and transported to the bone marrow, where it stimulates the production of red blood cells, the cells that transport oxygen (for more on the function of red blood cells, see the Cardiovascular System section later in this chapter).

The effects of hormones are countless and far-reaching. They are responsible for the growth of every cell and tissue in the body, including skeletal muscle. Specific hormones control metabolic rate, blood volume, and the breakdown and storage of glycogen, fats, and proteins. There are so many hormones controlling the function of our bodies that listing all of them is well beyond the scope of this book. However, what follows is a list of the hormones that play the most prevalent roles in exercise performance.

Growth hormone. As can be deduced from its name, the primary effect of growth hormone is to stimulate cell growth. The many affected tissues include muscle and bone. Other actions of growth hormone, which is secreted by the pituitary gland, include mobilizing fat stores for energy use and decreasing the rate of glucose (glycogen) consumption.

Testosterone. The predominant male sex hormone, testosterone is secreted primarily by the testes but also by adrenal cortex glands on the kidneys (the principal source of testosterone in women). In addition to promoting the development of male primary and secondary sex characteristics (such as deepening of the voice and baldness), testosterone, along with growth hormone, stimulates growth of muscle and other tissues. Because of its potent effect in promoting muscle growth, testosterone is used (via injection) by athletes in many sports to build muscle mass and to repair muscle tissue damaged by strenuous training.

Insulin. Insulin is secreted by the pancreas in response to a meal. Its primary purpose is to stimulate muscle cells to consume nutrients like carbohydrates and proteins. When these nutrients are absorbed from the intestine into the bloodstream, insulin is released, allowing the muscle cells to absorb nutrients and use them for energy or to perform other metabolic activities.

Like growth hormone and testosterone, insulin plays an important role in building and repairing muscle tissue by allowing proteins to enter cells. Once inside, these proteins can be used for *anabolism* (building) of muscle tissue.

Glucagon. In many ways, glucagon, also secreted by the pancreas, acts in opposition to insulin. During periods of exercise, glucagon breaks down glycogen into glucose so it can be burned as energy. It also stimulates the synthesis of glucose from lactic acid and proteins, again to provide energy for the working muscle.

Cortisol. Cortisol is secreted by the adrenal cortex in response to injury or other physiological or psychological stress. It exerts control over a wide number of physiological processes varying from the maintenance of red blood cells to the inhibition of swelling following injury. However, for the exercising athlete, the two most important actions of cortisol are the control of enzymes that regulate carbohydrate metabolism and the mobilization of amino acids from muscle tissue.

In the presence of cortisol, enzymes that stimulate *gluconeogenesis*, the production of glucose from noncarbohydrate sources (see Protein Metabolism section in chapter 2), are activated, and those that catalyze *glycolysis*, the first step in the energy pathway that consumes carbohydrate (see Carbohydrate Metabolism section in chapter 2), are inhibited. These effects conserve the body's carbohydrate supplies and increase the amount of excercise that can be performed before exhaustion.

Cortisol stimulates the breakdown of muscle tissue and inhibits muscle growth. Although these effects seem to be detrimental, the ability to mobilize amino acids from muscle tissue allows cortisol to exert control over many physiological functions that affect athletic performance. During exercise, mobilized amino acids can be converted into carbohydrate by gluconeogenesis. The free amino acids also play an important role in maintaining blood volume and pressure during exercise.

Following exercise, continued mobilization of amino acids increases their numbers in the blood, making more amino acids available for the repair of muscle tissue damaged during exercise. Thus, cortisol provides one of the vital first steps in the repair of muscle tissue that leads to muscle growth.

Because of its role in the breakdown of muscle tissue, cortisol has been implicated as a possible contributor to overtraining. This supposition has led to the development of supplements that inhibit the release of cortisol. However, because of the many beneficial actions of cortisol, inhibiting its release during exercise may have detrimental effects. For more information on this, see the Phosphatidylserine section in chapter 10.

Adrenaline. Also known as *epinephrine*, this hormone is released by the adrenal glands during physical exercise. Adrenaline helps prepare the body to meet the demands of physical exercise by mobilizing energy sources. It mobilizes fats from fat stores and provides carbohydrate by breaking down muscle and liver glycogen into glucose. These energy substrates then can be transported to the working muscle and used to fuel muscular contractions. Adrenaline also increases the heart rate and the strength of the heart's contractions, thereby increasing the flow of blood to the working muscle. Finally, adrenaline causes the constriction of blood vessels that feed many of the body's organs and nonworking muscles, increasing the amount of blood available to working muscles.

Erythropoietin. Secreted by the kidneys, erythropoietin (EPO) stimulates the production of red blood cells, thereby increasing the oxygen-carrying capacity of the blood. Specialized oxygen-sensing cells in the kidneys trigger EPO production when blood oxygen levels are low. Any number of situations can cause a drop in blood oxygen levels and a subsequent release of EPO. During heavy exercise, for example, blood is shunted away from the kidneys and to the working muscle, where much of the oxygen is consumed. This response results in a reduction in the amount of oxygen delivered to the kidney and in an increase in the release of EPO. Exposure to high altitude can also increase EPO production, as the body has difficulty maintaining blood oxygen levels in the thin air of high-altitude environments (see Altitude Training and Alternatives in chapter 10). Due to its ability to increase red blood cell levels and the blood's oxygen-carrying capacity, using synthetic EPO has become a very popular—although illegal and dangerous—method of increasing athletic performance.

Cardiovascular System

The cardiovascular system consists of the heart and all the blood vessels that carry blood throughout the body. The blood flowing through the cardiovascular system transports nutrients and waste products. During exercise, the blood delivers fat, carbohydrate, and protein to the working muscle, where they can be converted into energy. The blood also delivers hormones such as insulin, testosterone, and EPO to their target tissues. Finally, blood is responsible for removing the waste products of metabolism.

Blood flows through a vast network of blood vessels consisting of arteries, veins, and capillaries. Arteries carry blood from the heart to the body's tissues. With the exception of the blood in the pulmonary artery, arterial blood is rich in oxygen and other nutrients. Veins carry blood from the peripheral tissues back to the heart, and venous blood is typically laden with the waste products of human metabolism. Besides transporting blood back to the heart, where it can be refortified with nutrients and then redistributed through the arteries, the

Five-time Tour de France champion Miguel Indurain benefited from an exceptionally high cardiovascular capacity.

veins are responsible for carrying blood to the tissues and organs that filter out and dispose of waste products.

Between the arteries and the veins are the capillaries. These are extremely small blood vessels (about 4 to 9 microns or about 0.0002 to 0.0004 inch across) with thin, porous walls that allow diffusion of nutrients and waste products. Capillaries permeate every living tissue system in the body. They carry blood deep into the lungs, where they dispose of carbon dioxide and pick up oxygen. They permeate the intestinal walls to allow the blood to absorb the nutrients used to feed the tissues of the body, and they saturate skeletal muscle to provide it with oxygen and energy substrates and to carry away the waste products of human metabolism.

The blood that flows through the arteries, capillaries, and veins is composed primarily of a water-based fluid called *plasma*. Within this fluid are a wide variety of cell types, each with a specific task or set of tasks that is vital to the survival of the organism. The most numerous of these cell types is the red blood cell. Red blood cells are responsible for carrying out a critical function of the exercising body—transporting oxygen to the working muscle, where it can be used to liberate energy.

Within each red blood cell are millions of *hemoglobin* molecules saturated with iron. Chemical attraction causes oxygen molecules to attach to the iron in the hemoglobin when the red blood cell passes through the lungs. The oxygen remains bound to the cell as it travels through the arteries and capillaries. When the cell reaches the muscle, the new environment causes oxygen to become less attracted to hemoglobin and more attracted to a molecule known as *myoglobin,* which is similar to hemoglobin except that it exists inside the muscle fibers. This allows the oxygen molecule to be transferred from the blood into the muscle, where it is used for energy metabolism.

The blood plays an extremely important role in exercise performance; even the slightest imbalance of one of its constituents can have a noticeable effect on an athlete's ability to perform work. For this reason, cyclists should undergo regular blood tests to monitor the health of their blood. For more information on blood testing and blood health, see Are Blood Tests Necessary? in chapter 3.

The physiological demands of track sprinting (right) are worlds apart from those of long-distance road racing (above). Despite the differences, both disciplines are fueled by the same energy source, ATP.

CHAPTER 2

Fuel for the Machine

During competition or heavy training, cyclists burn a lot of calories, so it's very important to ensure that nutritional needs are met. In addition to taking in adequate calories, cyclists need to consume a wide variety of nutrients to maintain good health and to extract the energy stored in the foods they eat. This chapter explains how food is processed into energy and how diet can affect exercise performance.

Energy Production

Three types of foods provide energy for working muscle—carbohydrates, fats, and proteins. Collectively, these nutrients are known as *macronutrients* because they are consumed in greater quantities than any other single nutrient (except for water). Carbohydrates and proteins provide about 4 Calories of energy per gram and fat about 9 Calories per gram. Once digested, each of these macronutrients undergoes a series of complex metabolic steps to be converted into *adenosine triphosphate,* or ATP, the compound solely responsible for providing energy to the body. No matter what type of activity is involved—short or long, easy or hard—ATP is the only compound that directly supplies the energy needed to complete our tasks. How an athlete's body converts food into ATP greatly affects exercise performance and thus should be of great concern to exercise physiologists, coaches, and athletes.

ATP Production

ATP, the energy source for all metabolic processes, is composed of an adenosine molecule bonded to three phosphate molecules. Each of the phosphates is attached to the adenosine molecule with a high-energy bond. To release energy, the body breaks one of these bonds, yielding adenosine diphosphate (ADP), free phosphate (P_i), and energy.

Despite its importance as a supply of energy, bodily stores of ATP are quite small and must be replenished constantly during exercise. This can be achieved in a number of ways. One method involves a molecule called creatine phosphate, which can donate its phosphate molecule to the depleted ADP molecule to form ATP and free creatine. This reaction has prompted scientists to test the effectiveness of supplementing the diet with free creatine to increase ATP resynthesis and improve energy levels. For more on creatine supplementation, see chapter 10.

Another way the body maintains ATP levels is by having an ADP molecule donate one of its remaining phosphates to another ADP molecule. This reaction produces one ATP and a molecule known as adenosine monophosphate, or AMP.

Finally, the body can use the foods we eat to generate ATP. Through several complex series of reactions, the body converts carbohydrates, fats, and proteins from our diets into energy that can be used as fuel for the exercising muscle.

Digestion and Metabolism of Macronutrients

Carbohydrates

Carbohydrates, the most versatile supplier of ATP, fuel virtually every metabolic process in the human body. All activities, from the most vigorous exercise to breathing and even thinking, require the energy supplied by carbohydrates. The most basic form of carbohydrate is sugar, which is considered a simple carbohydrate because of its simple structure. Common forms of simple sugars are glucose, fructose (commonly found in fruits), and sucrose (table sugar), which is made by combining glucose and fructose. Complex carbohydrates such as breads, cereals, and pasta are formed by combining many molecules of simple carbohydrates, such as glucose, into a structure known as a *polymer.*

The body stores large amounts of carbohydrates as glycogen to ensure that supplies of this important energy substrate are readily available. Glycogen, formed through the combination of thousands of glucose molecules, is stockpiled primarily in the liver, the body's central storage depot, and in skeletal muscle. Whenever a part of the body requires carbohydrate, liver glycogen can be broken down into glucose, released into the bloodstream, transported to the appropriate location, and used as energy. In contrast, muscle glycogen cannot be released from its storage site in the muscle; it is used within that particular muscle to fuel muscular contractions and other processes.

Is There a Difference between the Types of Sugars?

Despite the wide variety of carbohydrates that can be utilized by the human body, the only form we can metabolize for energy is glucose. Fortunately, the body is able to convert many types of carbohydrates into glucose. Once carbohydrates are absorbed from the intestine, they are transported to the liver, where the conversion takes place. The glucose can then be released into the blood for transport to target tissues or retained by the liver to make liver glycogen.

Different carbohydrates are absorbed in different ways from the intestine. Molecules called glucose carriers, found in the wall of the intestine, attach to glucose molecules on the inside of the intestine and carry them to the outer wall, speeding the absorption of molecules into the bloodstream. Interestingly, during this process, the glucose carrier simultaneously transports a water molecule. As you might suspect, this mechanism aids in water absorption and is an important consideration in the formulation of sports drinks. (For more on sports drinks, see chapter 10.) Conversely, there is no carrier for fructose; it is left to passively travel across the wall of the small intestine to be absorbed. The net result is that glucose can be absorbed more quickly and enters the bloodstream at a faster rate than fructose. As for sucrose, it is broken down into glucose and fructose in the small intestine and the components are absorbed as just described.

Fats

Fats come from two sources, vegetable fats that commonly exist as oils and animal fats that exist in solid forms such as lard or tallow. Regardless of the source, fats are made up of *triglycerides*. A triglyceride is a compound composed of a glycerol molecule to which are attached three long carbon chains called *fatty acids*. Upon digestion, the fatty acids are separated from the glycerol and absorbed as *free fatty acids* (FFAs). Once absorbed, FFAs are transported to the liver, where they are combined with cholesterol and re-released into the bloodstream for transport to storage sites (body fat). Once the fat-cholesterol complex reaches the storage site, it is converted back into and stored as a triglyceride.

Unlike carbohydrates, which can be digested quickly, fats are digested and absorbed slowly. Fat metabolism is also considerably more complex than carbohydrate metabolism, meaning fats cannot provide quick energy for working muscle. Furthermore, the body requires more oxygen to extract energy from fat than from carbohydrate. Thus, fat is used only sparingly during high-intensity exercise when oxygen is at a premium.

The advantage of fat as an energy source lies in its immense storage capacity. When packed to the brim, the human body can store only 2,000 to 2,500 Calories as glycogen. By comparison, even the leanest cyclist stores roughly 30,000 Calories in his fat tissue. And while 1 gram of carbohydrate provides 4 Calories, 1 gram of fat provides 9. Likewise, 1 molecule of carbohydrate can produce 36 ATP molecules, while 1 FFA molecule produces approximately 130. So, although fat cannot fuel high-intensity activities, it can provide many of the calories required during the long, moderately intense efforts of a road race, conserving the limited carbohydrate stores for intense efforts like breakaways and sprinting.

Proteins

Proteins consist of smaller units known as *amino acids*. Although the body can make the majority of the amino acids it needs, there are seven amino acids, known as *essential amino acids*, that the body cannot make and must consume in the diet. Once consumed, proteins are broken down into amino acids and absorbed into the bloodstream. From there, the amino acids can be reassembled into the specific proteins the body requires.

Proteins carry out a host of functions vital to athletic performance. Probably the most widely known use for proteins is to provide the building blocks for muscle tissue. However, proteins provide the structure for virtually every soft tissue in the body, with the exception of adipose tissue. Proteins are also the major components of enzymes and hormones, which regulate many physiological processes, and special blood proteins help regulate blood volume. Finally, proteins can be broken down into amino acids and used as an energy source. While some amino acids can provide a direct source of ATP, others can be converted into glucose and burned as carbohydrate.

Like carbohydrates, proteins supply 4 Calories of energy per gram. However, compared to fats and carbohydrates, relatively little is known about the contribution of protein in meeting energy demands since proteins are difficult to track once consumed. While science has devised relatively simple techniques to measure fat and carbohydrate metabolism, no such simple methods exist for proteins. However, the use of certain complicated methods does allow for a more thorough understanding of how proteins contribute to the structure and function of the human body.

During exercise, the body must supply energy to the working muscle and vital internal organs. While carbohydrates and fats contribute the vast majority of energy to the working muscle, proteins also can be used to provide fuel. During exercise, proteins are taken from major storage sites like the blood and nonworking muscle. They are broken down into amino acids and then transported to either the working muscle, where they can be burned for energy, or the liver, where they are converted into glucose.

Once exercise has ceased, the body continues to mobilize proteins, mainly from the blood, to repair any muscle tissue damaged during exercise and to replace proteins used for fuel. Protein consumed in the diet is then used to replenish blood protein levels and provide amino acids for structural maintenance of muscle and other tissues.

Energy Pathways

Carbohydrates, fats, and proteins must be converted into ATP, the body's energy provider, before they can fuel metabolic processes. A number of metabolic pathways convert foods into ATP. Some of these pathways process only one of the three substrates, while others are common pathways through which all foods travel.

Carbohydrate Metabolism

Carbohydrate, or more specifically glucose, is the most versatile energy source available to the human body because it can be burned with or without oxygen. Glucose is stored in the body in two forms: as free glucose in the blood, commonly known as blood sugar; and as glycogen in the liver and skeletal muscle. Once in the muscle cell, glucose enters *glycolysis*, an *anaerobic* (without oxygen) metabolic pathway that can break down glucose quickly and provide an immediate source of ATP. The net gain from burning 1 molecule of glucose via glycolysis is 2 molecules of ATP and 1 molecule of *pyruvic acid*.

Under proper conditions, pyruvic acid is transported into the mitochondria of the muscle cell, where it is converted into acetyl-CoA. Acetyl-CoA then enters an energy pathway known as the *Krebs cycle*, where it undergoes a number of transformations and produces substrates consumed in a third metabolic pathway, the *electron transport chain*. Here, these Krebs cycle substrates are combined with oxygen in chemical reactions that produce ATP. Because oxygen is involved, the electron transport chain is commonly referred to as the *aerobic* pathway.

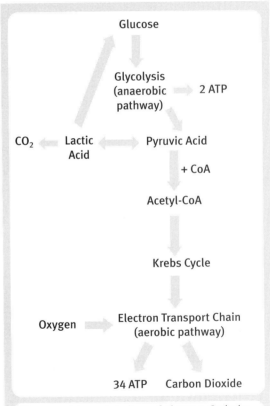

Glucose

Glycolysis (anaerobic pathway) → 2 ATP

CO_2 ← Lactic Acid ⇄ Pyruvic Acid

+ CoA

Acetyl-CoA

Krebs Cycle

Oxygen → Electron Transport Chain (aerobic pathway)

34 ATP   Carbon Dioxide

The complete metabolism of glucose. Carbohydrate is the only energy source that can provide quick energy through the anaerobic pathway (glycolysis). The aerobic pathway for glucose metabolism can provide far more ATP than glycolysis, but it cannot respond to quick increases in energy needs.

For every molecule of pyruvic acid produced by glycolysis and consumed by the electron transport chain, 34 ATP molecules are produced. Thus when 1 molecule of glucose is completely consumed by glycolysis, the Krebs cycle, and the electron transport chain, a total of 36 ATP molecules are produced, 34 from pyruvic acid and 2 from glucose.

Unfortunately, the capacities of the Krebs cycle and electron transport chain are limited. Because the Krebs cycle substrates must be combined with oxygen in the electron transport chain, the rate at which the electron transport chain can produce energy is limited by the availability of oxygen. A second limiting factor of the aerobic pathway is the availability of the enzymes that catalyze its reactions. Early in exercise, before adequate amounts of oxygen can be supplied to the aerobic pathway, or during high-intensity exercise, when glycolysis produces pyruvic acid at a faster rate than it can be consumed, pyruvic acid begins to accumulate. At this point, pyruvic acid is converted to the well-known and oft-vilified *lactic acid,* also known as *lactate.* More information on the effects of lactic acid on carbohydrate metabolism and exercise performance will be presented later in this chapter in the Carbohydrates, Oxygen, and Lactate Threshold section.

Fat Metabolism

Fats are stored as triglycerides in our adipose tissue, liver, and muscle tissue. Triglycerides consist of a glycerol molecule connected to three fatty acid chains, giving rise to its name.

When the need for energy arises, the fatty acid chains are removed from the glycerol base, forming free fatty acids that are released into the bloodstream and transported to the working muscle. Once inside the muscle cell, the FFAs are transported into the mitochondria

(the site of the aerobic pathway) and broken down in a process known as *beta-oxidation.* During beta-oxidation, the FFAs are broken into several two-carbon units and combined with a molecule of CoA to form acetyl-CoA, which is then consumed by the Krebs cycle and the electron transport chain in the same manner as the acetyl-CoA formed from pyruvic acid.

Because there is no fast-acting anaerobic en-

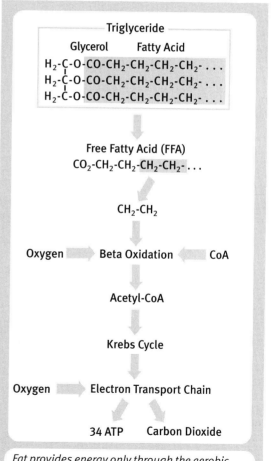

Fat provides energy only through the aerobic pathway and is not a quick source of ATP. However, fat can supply an enormous number of calories and is the preferred energy source during exercise performed below maximal steady state.

ergy pathway for fats, they cannot be called upon to provide quick energy for the working muscle. Furthermore, the significantly more complex pathway through which fat must be metabolized limits how fast it can supply ATP to the working muscle.

Protein Metabolism

While proteins provide only a small amount of the energy required for most exercise, they can become a significant source of energy during prolonged workouts or when glycogen stores become depleted. When proteins are mobilized during exercise, they are degraded into amino acids and transported to the working muscle or the liver. In the working muscle, amino acids are further degraded into the familiar two-carbon units which, like fats, are combined with CoA to form acetyl-CoA. The acetyl-CoA is then consumed by the Krebs cycle and electron transport chain. Thus, like fat, which also lacks an anaerobic pathway, these amino acids cannot supply quick energy to the exercising muscle.

Another fate awaits those amino acids transported to the liver. Through a complex series of steps, the liver converts some types of amino acids into glucose. This process, *gluconeogenesis*, or the creation of glucose from noncarbohydrate sources, is vital to maintaining glucose supplies during prolonged exercise. Glucose created by gluconeogenesis then can be released into the bloodstream, delivered to the exercising muscle, and metabolized like any other glucose molecule.

Carbohydrates, Oxygen, and Lactate Threshold

The concept of *lactate threshold* (also mistakenly known as *anaerobic threshold*) has been a

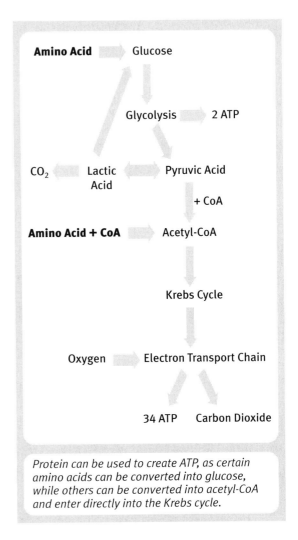

Protein can be used to create ATP, as certain amino acids can be converted into glucose, while others can be converted into acetyl-CoA and enter directly into the Krebs cycle.

focus of endurance training for a number of years. A lactate threshold test can be performed in almost any exercise physiology lab and involves monitoring the blood lactate levels of a cyclist as he or she rides at progressively higher workloads. At each level, a blood sample is taken and analyzed for lactate. As the exercise intensity increases, so does the rate of lactate production. Eventually, lactate is produced in such great quantities that it begins to accumulate in the blood. When this point—the lactate threshold—is reached, the test administrator notes the workload and the heart rate at which it occurs. This information can be used to prescribe workout intensity and effectively monitor training progress.

Lactic acid's relationship with exercise performance makes it a common topic for discussion among competitive cyclists and coaches alike. However, this relationship is one of the most poorly understood concepts in competitive cycling. Lactic acid is a by-product of glycolysis, the burning of carbohydrate in the absence of oxygen. When pyruvic acid is produced by glycolysis, it faces one of two metabolic fates (see illustration, page 16). Ideally, it enters the aerobic pathway and produces ATP. However, the capacity of the aerobic pathway to consume pyruvic acid is limited by the availability of both oxygen and the enzymes that catalyze the pathway's metabolic reactions. During rest and moderate exercise, this capacity is not challenged, and most of the pyruvic acid produced by glycolysis is consumed by the aerobic pathway. However, during heavy exercise, the rate of glycolysis is increased in an attempt to provide more ATP for the working muscle, producing pyruvic acid in amounts that exceed the aerobic pathway's capacity to consume it. Under these conditions, the excess pyruvic acid is quickly degraded into lactic acid. Lactic acid has many fates, and while commonly considered to be a harmful waste product, it has many necessary and even positive functions for the endurance athlete. But before we consider the beneficial roles of lactic acid, let's take a closer look at how it is involved in the concept of lactate threshold.

Newly produced lactic acid quickly degrades into lactate, which is transported out of the muscle cell and into the blood for disposal. As exercise intensity increases, so does lactic acid production, resulting in greater amounts of lactate entering the blood. When the rate of lactate production exceeds the rate of lactate disposal, significant amounts of the compound begin to accumulate in the blood, and lactate threshold is reached.

So what does lactate threshold have to do with exercise performance? Typically, lactate threshold is associated with the highest work rate a person can maintain for an extended period of time without fatiguing, a concept known as *maximal steady state,* or MSS. The power output at which MSS occurs is a person's *maximum sustainable power output,* or MSPO. The higher a person's MSPO, the greater the amount of work that person can do in a given time period, which ultimately translates to higher speed.

To improve their ability to produce and sustain high power outputs, cyclists must train at or above their maximum sustainable power output. Determining a person's MSPO and heart rate at MSPO allows training intensities to be prescribed more precisely, leading to a more effective training program. Unfortunately, many coaches and athletes training to improve MSPO make the mistake of prescribing exercise intensity based on percentage of maximum heart rate. This method is inappropriate, because heart rate at MSPO does not occur at the same percentage of maximal heart rate in all individuals. Thus, while training at 85 percent of maximal heart rate may provide one individual with the optimum intensity for increasing her MSPO, it may be above or below the proper training intensity for another. Therefore, cyclists should use a field or laboratory test to determine their MSPO and heart rate at MSPO (for more information, see chapter 3).

Why do lactic acid and lactate play such influential roles in MSS and MSPO? During lactic acid's conversion to lactate, it releases hydrogen ions, which wreak havoc on many metabolic processes in muscle cells. Much like lactate, these hydrogen ions are transported from the muscle cells into the bloodstream where they are neutralized by buffering agents. However, during intense excercise when lactic acid (and hydrogen ion) production is excessive, hydrogen ions accumulate in the muscle, which inhibits glycolysis, hinders energy production, and interferes with the mechanical aspects of muscle contraction. In short, the accumulation of hydrogen ions can stop an athlete from performing all but the lightest of exercise. Thus, when sports scientists measure blood lactate during a lactate threshold test, they are looking at blood lactate levels only as an indirect indicator of hydrogen levels in the muscle.

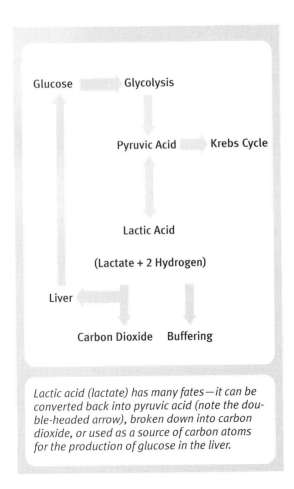

Lactic acid (lactate) has many fates—it can be converted back into pyruvic acid (note the double-headed arrow), broken down into carbon dioxide, or used as a source of carbon atoms for the production of glucose in the liver.

Fates of Lactate

The accumulation of lactate itself, whether in the blood or muscle, has never been shown to restrict exercise performance. In fact, lactate can benefit exercising athletes. One benefit is its conversion back into pyruvate (the acid salt of pyruvic acid), which can then be burned via the aerobic pathway. During periods when lactate is produced in large quantities, it can be transported via the blood to the heart or other muscle tissue, where it is converted back into pyruvate. The pyruvate can then be converted into acetyl-CoA and consumed by the Krebs cycle. This process spares glycogen in these tissues by providing pyruvate without the further breakdown of glycogen.

Lactate also can be transported to the liver and used to form glucose via gluconeogenesis. This newly formed glucose can be released into the blood and transported back to the working muscle, where it once again can be burned for energy. In effect, through the production of lactic acid, the body can recycle its glycogen stores!

Exercise Metabolism: Putting It All Together

The combination of three energy substrates and a number of metabolic pathways makes exercise metabolism a complex subject for the scientist. However, for the competitive cyclist, understanding exercise metabolism and learning to use it to your advantage can be relatively simple if you remember that, generally, the body will first use the most readily available energy substrate unless that substrate cannot meet the energy demand. In such a case, the body will switch to an alternative energy source. For instance, early in an exercise session carbohydrate is the preferred source of energy. Although fat and protein stores are substantially more abundant, the processes of converting these substrates to ATP are slower and more complicated. Because glycogen is stored in close proximity to the working muscle fibers, unlike fats and proteins, it can be rapidly broken down and easily burned for energy.

After thirty to forty-five minutes of exercise, fat is mobilized and becomes a more prevalent energy source. In fact, during prolonged, moderate-intensity exercise, fat is the predominant source of energy. However, whenever exercise becomes vigorous (at or above lactate threshold), carbohydrate once again replaces fat as the predominant energy source. There are two reasons for this. First, during intense exercise oxygen supplies are at a premium, and because carbohydrate is the only energy substrate that can provide ATP without oxygen, the body utilizes its carbohydrate stores more readily. Second, since vigorous exercise burns ATP rapidly, the body relies on carbohydrate because it can supply ATP faster than can fat or protein. Because carbohydrate is such an important energy source for vigorous exercise, when carbohydrate stores become depleted, the ability to perform high-intensity exercise becomes extremely limited and often nonexistent. Cyclists commonly refer to this situation as bonking.

Proteins become involved as energy providers after about an hour of continuous exercise. At this point, the body may have consumed a significant amount of its vital carbohydrate stores and must be concerned with conserving its remaining glycogen. However, while protein can help conserve glycogen stores by reducing the exercising muscles' demand for carbohydrates and by being converted into glucose, these steps can only delay the inevitable as glucose demand during exercise far outpaces the body's ability to provide it through gluconeogenesis.

Macronutrient Needs

Research investigating the effects on exercise performance of consuming different amounts and ratios of carbohydrates, fats, and proteins has been exhaustive. While the results from these studies are well known to many members of the scientific community, some supplement manufacturers have put interesting spins on the data to help sell their products. Wild claims of weight loss, weight gain, higher energy levels, and improved performance are disseminated throughout the media. Yet these extravagant claims can also be persuasive, and I'm fairly sure that the average consumer—who doesn't have a physiology or nutrition degree—usually doesn't stand a chance of making an informed decision.

Most athletes can meet their nutritional needs easily and inexpensively. While there are a number of specially formulated products on the market that will benefit performance, many products offer no advantage or are overkill for the competitive athlete. Knowing which products are worth the money and which are not is simply a matter of knowing the nutritional requirements of an athlete.

Carbohydrate and Fat Consumption

In the 1980s, sports scientists had great interest in the idea of improving exercise performance by consuming a diet rich in carbohydrates. Their reasoning seemed sound; fatigue in endurance exercise is highly correlated with depletion of glycogen stores, carbohydrates are burned in great amounts during vigorous exercise, and glycogen stores are limited. Numerous well-controlled studies measuring the effects of various types of diets on glycogen levels and exercise performance concluded that a diet high in carbohydrate is superior to high-fat or high-protein diets. It seemed that the question of optimal diet composition had been settled.

Recently, however, there has been a backlash against the accepted high-carbohydrate diet by a few "scientists" and a number of nutritional supplement manufacturers who have suggested that a diet higher in fat can reduce body fat, increase oxygen consumption, and improve exercise performance. Although these high-fat proponents make many persuasive arguments in their books and advertisements, much of the research used to support these beliefs is poorly performed, and the data from other studies are improperly manipulated in order to support their claims.

The claim that a higher-fat diet can reduce body fat and weight is supported by the observation that when a person follows such a diet, he burns more fat during rest and moderate exercise than when adhering to a diet high in carbohydrate. While this is true, the individual is nevertheless also consuming more fat, and as long as he is in caloric balance, his body fat levels do not appear to change significantly.

Supporters of the high-fat diet also point out that the body's storage capacity for carbohydrate is limited and that excess carbohydrates consumed on a high-carbohydrate diet are converted to and stored as fat. While the first half of this statement is true, the validity of the second half is questionable. Rats and other lower mammals have shown the ability to convert carbohydrates into fats, but thus far, studies designed to induce and observe this ability in humans have been unsuccessful. Regardless of whether humans are capable of making the conversion, simple math makes it obvious that it is better to overconsume carbohydrates than to overconsume fats. Converting carbohydrates into fat is an energy-consuming process. While the process of creating 1 pound of stored body fat from dietary fat con-

sumes about 3,600 Calories, creating 1 pound of stored body fat from dietary carbohydrates consumes about 4,200 Calories. Thus, an extra 600 Calories could be consumed without any appreciable weight gain if the Calories are consumed as carbohydrates as opposed to fat.

The claim that increased fat consumption results in an increase in oxygen consumption is backed by substantial scientific evidence. Unfortunately, however, this increase in oxygen consumption does not lead to an improvement in exercise performance. The metabolic process of producing ATP from fat requires more oxygen than producing the same number of ATP molecules from carbohydrate. Thus, when fat consumption and utilization rise, exercising oxygen consumption also rises but with no improvement in exercise performance.

Finally, while a number of well-designed studies have shown improvements in exercise performance from high-fat diets, most of these studies have been performed on rats. As a professor of mine once told me, "Rats aren't humans, but some humans are rats!" And unfortunately, the results from many of these studies have been mistakenly generalized to humans. Rats are able to utilize fat stores more effectively than humans, and rats actually perform exercise tasks better after fasting or when they are in a glycogen-depleted state. Humans, on the other hand, perform much better with full glycogen stores and/or after a high-carbohydrate meal. The plain fact is that no well-designed research studies have been published showing improvements in exercise performance when endurance athletes forgo a carbohydrate-rich diet for one that is high in fat.

Protein Consumption

Although protein provides only a small percentage of the energy required for exercise, it is essential for a number of important processes that affect the performance of competitive cyclists, such as the maintenance of muscle tissue, hormones, and enzymes. The current recommended dietary allowance (RDA) for protein is 0.8 gram of protein per kilogram of body weight (about 0.4 gram per pound) per day. Although there has been much speculation about whether athletes have increased protein needs, the answers have been hard to come by because of the difficulty of measuring protein requirements. However, a few studies have suggested that endurance athletes, because of their reliance on protein as an energy source, may have protein requirements as much as twice the RDA. Some studies have indicated that during periods of heavy training, runners and cyclists are unable to meet their protein needs until they consume 1.5 grams of protein per kilogram of body weight per day. Before I start a stampede on the meat markets and supplement stores, let me caution you that it is not difficult to consume 1.5 grams of protein per kilogram body weight. Unless you are a strict vegetarian, you probably already are consuming that much protein in your daily diet.

Most individuals can get fairly accurate estimates of their protein consumption by reading food labels and keeping track of what they eat. If you are a vegetarian or are concerned about your daily protein intake you may want to contact a registered dietitian who can perform a dietary analysis. Be forewarned, however, that if the dietitian is not familiar with the research on increased protein requirements of endurance athletes, he or she may unintentionally misinform you about your protein status. Thus, you should learn your actual daily protein intake rather than being satisfied with the news that your intake is "sufficient."

In addition to the arguments over the amount of protein needed by endurance athletes, there also has been much debate over when protein should be consumed. Many individuals in the supplement industry have argued that large quantities of protein should be consumed immediately after exercise to aid in the replacement of proteins catabolized for energy and to help repair damaged muscle tissue. However, the body has vast protein stores and is well equipped to handle the initial complications of increased protein demand brought on by exercise. Furthermore, the process of rebuilding damaged muscle tissue can take several days to complete. Thus, if the body is supplied with adequate dietary protein, muscle repair will likely proceed unfettered regardless of when the protein is consumed.

However, there may yet be an advantage to consuming protein immediately after exercise. A fair amount of evidence indicates that when athletes consume protein with carbohydrates after exercise, they may be able to replenish their glycogen stores more quickly and completely than when they consume only carbohydrates. While all studies have not shown this positive effect, the consumption of protein after exercise does not appear to have any detrimental effects.

General Recommendations for Macronutrient Consumption

By now, you may be thoroughly confused about the optimal composition of fats, proteins, and carbohydrates in your diet. Despite all of the complicated research, you can ensure adequate intake of these dietary components by following three simple rules.

• During periods of racing and heavy training, consume 8 to 10 grams of carbohydrate per kilogram of body weight per day. Research has demonstrated that athletes who are undertaking heavy training loads can maintain their glycogen levels by consuming this amount. If you are tapering, continue to consume these quantities to ensure high glycogen levels going into competition. If your training is not particularly heavy, 5 to 6 grams of carbohydrate per kilogram of body weight is probably sufficient.

Interestingly, studies show that when athletes consume more than 10 grams of carbohydrate per kilogram per day, glycogen levels increase no further. This suggests that there is an upper limit to glycogen storage capacity that is satisfied by a daily intake of 10 grams per kilogram. Remember to include carbohydrates that are consumed during exercise in the form of energy bars, gels, and sports drinks when determining your daily carbohydrate consumption.

- Consume approximately 1.5 grams of protein per kilogram of body weight each day.
- Meet the remainder of your caloric requirements with fats and/or carbohydrates.

During periods of hard training and competition, cyclists can burn extraordinary amounts of calories. Racers competing in the Tour de France have been shown to burn over 5,000 Calories per day during competition, although this is an extreme example. The average competitive cyclist probably burns about 3,000 to 4,000 Calories in a day's work, with women, on average, burning less than men.

Micronutrient Needs

Micronutrients, which include vitamins and minerals, are so called because they are required in much smaller amounts than macronutrients. However, these nutrients perform a wide variety of tasks necessary to sustain life as well as allow optimal athletic performance.

Vitamins

Since their discovery in the early part of the twentieth century, vitamins have been one of the most-studied components of human nutrition. The primary function of many vitamins is to act as *coenzymes* that help catalyze thousands of chemical reactions in the body. Although vitamins do not provide energy in the form of calories, the coenzymes formed from B vitamins catalyze many of the energy-releasing reactions of glycolysis and the aerobic energy pathway. Thus, a person who has a deficiency of B vitamins may feel lethargic even though he or she is consuming an adequate number of calories. Many vitamins contribute to the competitive cyclist's performance, but a complete review is beyond the scope of this book. However, the functions of some of the more important vitamins are discussed below.

Vitamin A. This vitamin helps maintain healthy skin, bones, and gums and is essential for proper vision. Vitamin A is commonly found in egg yolks, milk, and green and yellow vegetables.

Vitamin B complex. This family of vitamins is important for the release of energy from carbohydrates, fats, and proteins. Common sources of B vitamins include milk, meat, grains, and cereals.

Vitamin C. Essential to the maintenance of healthy teeth, gums, bones, and blood vessels, vitamin C also plays vital roles in the immune system, hormone synthesis, and iron absorption and acts as an antioxidant. Sources of vitamin C include citrus fruits, potatoes, and tomatoes.

Vitamin E. This vitamin protects cell membranes from oxidation by acting as a powerful antioxidant. Sources of vitamin E include vegetable oils, eggs, meat, and fish.

Minerals

Numerous essential minerals perform a variety of functions in the human body, and many perform several duties. Minerals are required to provide structure to bone tissue, to allow the contraction and relaxation of muscle, and to maintain proper levels of hydration. Some of the more important minerals are the following.

Calcium. The major mineral that gives integrity to bones and teeth, calcium also is required for muscular contractions as well as the function of some enzymes. Sources of calcium include milk and other dairy products, clams, sardines, and salmon.

Magnesium. This mineral acts in opposition to calcium in the process of muscular relaxation. Deficiency of magnesium can result in muscular cramping and local muscular fatigue. Magnesium also is required to activate many of the enzymes involved in the energy-releasing pathways. Vegetables, meat, and seafood are excellent sources of magnesium.

Sodium. An essential mineral in the regulation of hydration, sodium also plays vital roles in muscular contraction, nerve function, and enzyme regulation. Sodium is found in almost all processed foods as well as table salt.

Potassium. Like sodium, potassium is essential to water balance and enzyme activity. Potassium is prevalent in fruits, vegetables, meats, and cereals.

Chloride. This mineral assists in fluid balance and the uptake of oxygen and carbon dioxide by red blood cells. Chloride can be found in abundance in table salt, meat, fish, and poultry.

Iron. A component of hemoglobin and myoglobin, iron is essential for the transport of oxygen to the working muscle. Good sources of iron include meat, eggs, dried fruit, and enriched breads and cereals.

Zinc. This mineral is an essential part of insulin, which helps transport proteins and carbohydrates into muscle cells. Zinc also is necessary for the digestion and synthesis of proteins and the maintenance of the immune system. Shellfish, seafood, liver, nuts, and milk are excellent sources of zinc.

Chromium. Chromium assists insulin in regulating blood glucose and transporting nutrients into cells. Because of its importance to the function of insulin, chromium supplementation recently has become popular for promoting muscle growth and encouraging the burning of fat tissue. Good sources of chromium include meat, seafood, and whole-grain breads and cereals. For more on chromium supplementation, see chapter 10.

Vitamin and Mineral Requirements for Cyclists

In the early part of the twentieth century, scientists began to study the dietary needs for vitamins and minerals. A great deal of research was and still is performed to determine the amounts of vitamins and minerals—the recommended dietary allowances (RDAs)—necessary to maintain good health. Over the last several years, debate (much of it perpetuated by the supplement industry) has centered on the adequacy of the current RDAs for competitive athletes. The rationale for this debate is that because athletes place much greater demands on their bodies, their vitamin and mineral needs are much greater than those of sedentary individuals.

In fact, some research has suggested that athletes may require higher doses of certain vitamins and minerals. However, there is no evidence that consuming megadoses of vitamins and minerals can improve athletic performance in healthy individuals. This is because the RDAs for vitamins and minerals are set with a large margin of error to accommodate special groups like athletes. For instance, to maintain good health the average active adult requires approximately 10 milligrams of vitamin C per day. However, the RDA for vitamin C has been set at 60 milligrams, six times higher than what most adults require! Thus, any increased needs by athletes for vitamins and minerals are likely already built into the current RDAs. Furthermore, it is relatively easy to consume the necessary amounts of vitamins and minerals just by taking in an adequate number of calories from a wide variety of foods (fruits, vegetables, grains, and meat). This is not to say that athletes do not require vitamin and mineral supplements. In fact, I recommend to all of my clients that they regularly take a multivitamin-mineral supplement. The reason I do this is that although cyclists and other endurance athletes consume large numbers of calories to meet their energy needs, these calories often come from a relatively narrow family of foods. As a result, their diets may lack the variety necessary to consistently supply adequate amounts of many important vitamins and minerals. You should be careful, however, not to use vitamin and mineral supplements as a crutch, because many beneficial compounds found in foods are not found in supplements. Thus, always strive to eat a wide variety of foods.

Another reason to consider supplementation (especially for women) is the need for iron, which plays an important role in the blood's ability to carry oxygen. When an iron-deficient diet is combined with heavy training loads, an individual is placed at risk for anemia, which can have a devastating effect on exercise performance. Women run an even greater risk for developing anemia because of the increased iron loss associated with menstrual bleeding. The RDA for iron is 12 milligrams per day for men and 18 milligrams per day for women. Although it is not impossible to consume these amounts in the diet, it can be difficult, especially if you don't regularly eat red meat. (For more on iron requirements and anemia, see chapter 3.) Thus, it is a good idea to consume a daily multivitamin-mineral supplement that includes the RDA for iron as a relatively inexpensive insurance policy against deficiencies of iron and other micronutrients.

Questions and Answers

Q. I have heard that many of the fruits and vegetables grown today have lower nutrient contents than in the past because overfarming has depleted nutrients from the soil. Is this true?
A. This is another myth perpetuated by some members of the supplement industry. The nutrient levels in the soil have very little to do with the nutritional value of the crops grown in that soil. Crops grown in nutrient-poor soil produce smaller and fewer fruits, but the nutritional value of the produce is the same as that grown in rich soils. For instance, apple trees growing in nutrient-poor soil produce fewer and smaller apples, but the nutritional value of those apples is not affected.

Q. Are the vitamins and minerals in supplements as good as those found in foods?
A. Structurally, there is no difference between the vitamins and minerals found in supplements and those found in foods. Once they are absorbed into the bloodstream, the body cannot tell the difference between vitamins and minerals produced naturally and those that are synthesized in a manufacturing plant. However, there is some evidence that the vitamins and minerals found in supplements may not be absorbed as readily as those found in food.

Q. What is the difference between lactate threshold and anaerobic threshold?

A. Essentially nothing. *Anaerobic threshold* was the original term used to describe the increase in blood lactate levels. The term *lactate threshold* is technically more correct, though, and thus has been adopted by most of the scientific community. However, both terms refer to the same event.

Q. I have noticed that some energy drinks contain lactate. Considering the negative effects of lactic acid, shouldn't cyclists avoid consuming lactate?

A. Not necessarily. Recall that lactate itself has no negative effect on exercise performance; the real culprit is the hydrogen released by lactic acid as it degrades into lactate. Lactate can actually be a useful energy source because it can be used to synthesize glucose or be converted into pyruvate. This conversion can be especially beneficial because it allows the body to produce pyruvate for aerobic energy production without using glycolysis. Thus, the addition of lactate can allow pyruvate to be produced without using glucose and without generating lactic acid.

Several years ago, researchers discovered that exercise performance could be improved if lactate was infused into the blood of exercising individuals. Unfortunately, the digestive tract is very intolerant of lactate, and when subjects were given similar amounts of lactate orally, they experienced side effects including severe abdominal cramps, diarrhea, and vomiting. People are able to tolerate lower dosages of lactate, but these dosages don't appear to be sufficient to improve exercise performance, even when the concentrations are twice the levels found in commercially available drinks.

The ability to maintain a high power output is especially important in time trials.

CHAPTER 3

Testing and Evaluation

Cyclists of all abilities can benefit from regular laboratory and field assessments. When I worked at the USOC and the USCF, we performed extensive laboratory tests on many athletes several times a year to help prescribe proper training loads and monitor training progress. Other tests, like the maximal oxygen consumption test, can be used to predict a competitive cyclist's potential for success. Without headwinds or tailwinds, cars or potholes, laboratories can control variables that could affect the outcome of your tests, and they have the equipment to measure your capabilities precisely and objectively. However, even if you can't visit an exercise physiology lab, you can still use stopwatches, Computrainers, heart rate monitors, and power meters to collect useful data in field tests. This chapter provides an explanation of field and laboratory tests that can provide insight into your current physical conditioning, potential for success, and optimal training loads.

Maximal Oxygen Consumption Test (VO$_2$ Max Test)

The VO$_2$ max test measures your body's ability to consume oxygen, and is expressed as milliliters of oxygen per kilogram of body weight per minute (mL/kg/min.). Because oxygen availability plays such a vital role in energy release, the amount of work a muscle can perform is limited by the amount of oxygen it can consume. Therefore, the greater a person's VO$_2$ max, the greater his or her potential for excelling in endurance sports like cycling.

Elite male road cyclists tend to have maximal oxygen consumption values in excess of 70 mL/kg/min. and some have values well over 90. Women tend to have lower values than men, typically in the high 50s to upper 60s. While training can improve a person's maximal oxygen consumption, the upper limit is determined genetically and usually is met after several months of hard training. Once they achieve their peak maximal oxygen consumption, athletes can maintain this level with only a moderate amount of high-intensity training. If they stop all high-intensity training, on the other hand, their VO$_2$ max will drop moderately. Because the primary purpose of determining maximal oxygen consumption is to gain insight into a person's potential for success in endurance sports, regular assessments are unnecessary. In fact, a single VO$_2$ max test at a time of high physical conditioning is probably all that is needed for most cyclists over the course of their competitive careers.

Performing a maximal oxygen consumption test involves riding at progressively higher workloads while your expired air is collected and analyzed. The test is performed on a specially designed bicycle ergometer that allows the technician to control your work rate. Your expired air is collected in a snorkel-like mouthpiece and transported through a hose to a metabolic cart, a collection of instruments that measure the amount of air you breathe, the amount of oxygen you extract from this air, and the amount of carbon dioxide you produce. A computer uses all of this information to calculate your oxygen consumption.

A subject begins a maximal oxygen consumption test by riding at a predetermined moderate work rate. The work rate is increased slightly (by about 25 watts or so) at regular intervals, usually one to three minutes. As the workload increases, the rider's muscles extract more and more oxygen from the blood to help satisfy the increasing energy demand. Eventually, the rider reaches a workload where the muscles' ability to extract oxygen from the blood peaks. At this point, further increases in workload will no longer elicit any increase in oxygen consumption and the rider has reached his or her highest possible level of oxygen consumption—VO_2 max. Soon afterward, the athlete will be overcome by the workload and become too exhausted to continue the test.

During a VO_2 max test, the subject rides at progressively higher workloads until he or she is completely exhausted. Expired air is collected through a hose in the mouth and analyzed to determine the amount of oxygen consumed.

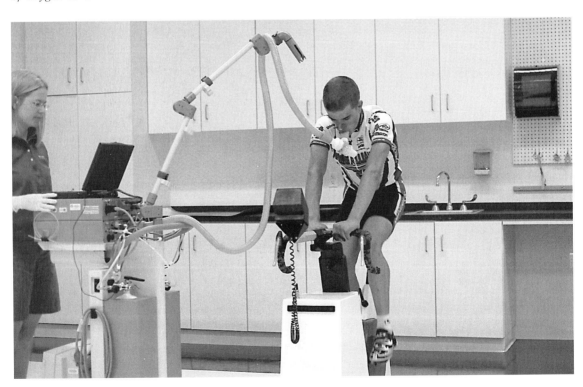

Lactate Threshold, Maximal Steady State, and Maximum Sustainable Power Output

The most important tests for endurance cyclists are evaluations of lactate threshold, maximal steady state (MSS), and maximum sustainable power output (MSPO). Recall from chapter 2 the significance of lactate threshold and energy metabolism. MSPO, or power output at MSS, is the highest power output a person can maintain for an extended period of time. *The ability to produce and maintain a high power output is the single most important physiological factor in determining the success of endurance cyclists.* All other things being equal, the rider with the highest power output at MSS will be the winner of the race simply because maintaining a higher power output translates into greater speed.

MSPO varies considerably depending on your training status, making it very useful for monitoring training progress and prescribing training intensity. Thus, you should perform MSS evaluations on a regular basis, particularly early in the year before you start interval training, before you start training to peak for a major event, or any time you want to know how a particular training block affects your MSPO.

Lactate Threshold

Evaluation of lactate threshold, MSS, and MSPO is a two-step process that begins with a lactate threshold test. This test involves riding the same type of ergometer used for the VO_2 max test. Again, the rider begins pedaling at a fairly light workload (typically 100 to 150 watts), and the workload is increased at a consistent rate, usually by 25 watts every three minutes. At the end of each three-minute stage, a small blood sample is drawn from the athlete's finger and analyzed for lactate concentration. As the test progresses, the increasing workload places greater demands on glycolysis (the lactate-producing energy system), increasing lactate production. During the early stages of the test, the body is able to dispose of the lactate as fast as it is produced, keeping blood lactate levels constant. However, at some

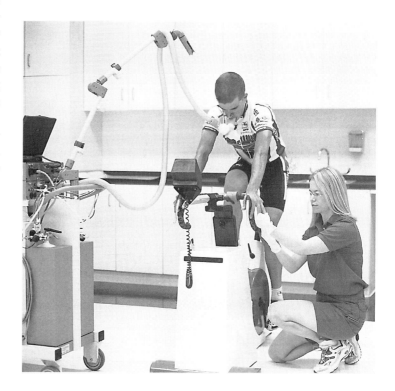

Professional cyclist Mike Creed performs a lactate threshold test in the exercise physiology lab at the U.S. Olympic Training Center. Blood is drawn from Mike's fingertip at regular intervals during the test and analyzed for lactate levels.

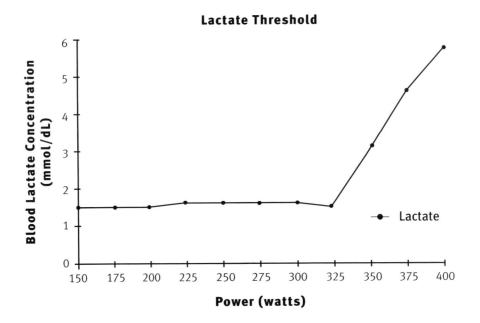

A graphical representation of a lactate threshold test. The significant rise in blood lactate concentration at 350 watts reveals that the rider has exceeded his lactate threshold of 325 watts.

point the escalating workload creates lactate too quickly for the body to process, causing a rise in blood lactate concentration and eventually resulting in a break in the lactate curve, the lactate threshold. The graph above represents the data from a lactate threshold test. The subject performed eleven stages of a progressive exercise test ranging in intensity from 150 to 400 watts. Notice that lactate levels stayed consistent from 150 to 325 watts. However, they increased significantly once the individual began riding at 350 watts, producing a break in the lactate curve. Thus, the rider's lactate threshold would be 325 watts.

Curves used to determine lactate threshold are not always neat and easy to interpret; sometimes a technician's subjective judgment is required. Furthermore, even the cleanest data from a lactate threshold test often under-

estimates a rider's MSPO. Thus, a more specific test needs to be performed to determine MSPO.

Maximum Sustainable Power Output

Once lactate threshold has been determined, a second test is needed to more precisely identify MSPO. While lactate threshold establishes the point where a metabolic shift causes an imbalance between lactate production and lactate consumption, it does not always identify the highest power output a rider can maintain for an extended period of time. To successfully identify MSPO, you must determine the effect of a particular workload on blood lactate concentration over time. Because a lactate threshold test only measures the concentration at one time point for each workload, it is difficult to predict whether a particular workload would be sustainable over an extended period. Consider the data used to create the lactate threshold graph shown opposite. A large rise in blood lactate concentration at a work rate of 350 watts caused a classic break in the lactate curve. This increase was greater than the 1 millimole (mmol) per deciliter (dL) standard commonly used to identify lactate threshold. Thus, the technician was correct in identifying the lactate threshold of 325 watts. However, when determining MSPO, the more important question is, how does this athlete's blood lactate respond to the current workload over an extended period of time? Just because the rider's blood lactate increased by more than 1 mmol/dL does not mean this workload is unsustainable. If this cyclist continues to ride at 350 watts without a further increase in blood lactate concentration, the workload is most likely sustainable and MSPO has not been exceeded. However, if the cyclist's blood lactate levels continue to climb, the workload is not sustainable and MSPO has been exceeded.

Testing for MSPO involves selecting several workloads below and above the established lactate threshold and riding at each of them for nine minutes. During each period, blood samples are obtained at minutes three, six, and nine and analyzed for lactate concentration. If the rider maintains a stable concentration at a given workload, she or he repeats the procedure at a slightly higher workload, continuing until the workload elicits an increase of greater than 1 mmol/dL in blood lactate between any of the three samples taken for that workload. For instance, for the rider in the example above, whose lactate threshold was determined to occur at a work rate of 325 watts, the MSPO test would start

just below lactate threshold and increase by 15 watts per stage. Thus, power output for the first stage would be 320 watts, followed by stages at 335 watts, 350 watts, etc. MSPO occurs at the highest power output that does not elicit a greater than 1 mmol/dL rise in blood lactate concentration between any of the three blood samples for a particular stage. This point in exercise metabolism is often referred to as *maximal steady state* because it is the highest workload a person can maintain while his or her lactate levels remain consistent, or in a steady state. Heart rate and power output at MSS (MSPO) should be recorded during the test, to be used later in prescribing training intensities.

Determining Maximum Sustainable Power Output without a Laboratory

If you don't have access to an exercise physiology lab or don't want to incur the expense of such testing, you can use a field test to gauge your MSS. You'll need your bicycle, a stationary trainer, a cadence meter, and a heart rate monitor. If you have a Computrainer, an SRM (see page 59), or some other device that allows you to monitor your power output, use it. The test is performed in a similar manner to the lactate threshold test in that it begins at a fairly low power output and gradually increases the workload. Stages are three minutes long, and you begin each stage by manually shifting into a larger gear or, if you are using a Computrainer, by increasing the workload by 20 watts. Continue the test until you reach the highest workload you believe you could maintain for an extended period of time, such as an hour. For competitive cyclists, this workload should be uncomfortable but not unbearable, equivalent to the intensity of a 40-kilometer time trial. Once you reach the required intensity, continue this stage for six minutes. Have a friend record your heart rate at minutes three, four, five, and six. If your heart rate at minute six is more than eight to ten beats per minute higher than it was at minute three, you are not in a steady state and have overshot your MSPO. Give yourself fifteen minutes of rest and repeat the test, reducing your final-stage intensity as needed. If the difference in heart rate between minutes three and six is less than eight beats per minute, you have likely found your MSS. Average the heart rates at minutes three, four, five, and six to obtain your MSS heart rate and record the power output for this final stage if it is available. These data will be used to prescribe proper exercise intensity in subsequent workouts.

A word of caution for those who use a stationary trainer: while work rate on a Computrainer is maintained regardless of cadence, on a stationary trainer it is dependent on cadence. Thus, you must maintain a consistent cadence for the duration of the test. Your actual cadence should be similar to what you use when you time trial, such as 80 to 100 rpm.

Wingate Anaerobic Test

This test was developed to assess an athlete's ability to perform work over a single maximal burst of high-intensity exercise. It typically measures peak power, average power, total work, and fatigue index, which is a measure of how quickly you fatigue over the course of the test. The Wingate test generally is used by track riders, who utilize short, high-power bursts of activity. However, road cyclists and mountain bikers frequently must produce short bursts of power during long competitions, making the Wingate test useful for them as well. Although not nearly as important for road and mountain bike racers as MSS tests, occasional Wingate

tests can help in evaluating the effects of certain types of intervals, like short (less than one minute), high-intensity intervals.

The Wingate test, performed on a bicycle ergometer outfitted with an SRM or some other device capable of measuring power and work, involves riding at the highest possible workload you can maintain for a given period of time (usually ten to thirty seconds). Because of the extremely high workload, you should undergo an extensive warm-up before beginning the test. You then start by pedaling at a predetermined cadence (usually 60 to 90 rpm) against very light resistance. The test begins with the addition of extra resistance (usually 7 to 9 percent of your body weight). Your objective is to reach and maintain your highest possible power output by pedaling as fast as you can for the duration of the test.

Male track sprinters are definitely the kings of the Wingate test and can produce as much as 2,000 watts of power for short periods of time. However, these riders also produce high fatigue indexes, as much as 60 to 70 percent, as they usually cannot maintain these high power outputs for more than a few seconds. Top road riders usually produce peak power outputs of 1,000 to 1,200 watts and have lower (usually 20 to 30 percent) fatigue indexes. Women cyclists have similar fatigue indexes, but their peak power outputs are generally 20 to 40 percent lower than those of their male counterparts.

Are Blood Tests Necessary?

Because the circulatory system transports so much vital cargo (hormones, nutrients, waste products), a blood test can help in evaluating the function of various organs and tissues as well as the nutritional status of the athlete. Regular blood tests can detect problems before symptoms arise and can provide baseline values

National team member Giddeon Massie performs a Wingate test. This procedure will help determine the efficacy of Giddeon's training by measuring his ability to produce power over a short time period.

to be used as future reference points. Blood tests should also be considered when athletes exhibit inexplicable fatigue, poor recovery, or declines in performance capacity. An annual blood test should be performed during the off-season, after a period of rest but before the athlete resumes heavy training. This strategy will provide data that are not skewed by the stress of hard training and will give a better indication of what to expect when the athlete is healthy and rested.

Blood is composed of watery liquid called *plasma* and solid matters dissolved in the plasma, collectively known as *hematocrit*. The hematocrit and its constituents are measured and expressed as concentrations, or amounts per unit of plasma. Because plasma is composed primarily of water, both plasma volume and the concentrations of the solids can be affected by a subject's hydration. Therefore, the subject should be properly hydrated before having blood drawn for analysis.

Blood Test Protocol

Blood tests should be performed following an overnight fast that is preceded by a rest day. This ensures that the test results will not reflect transient changes in blood chemistry resulting from strenuous exercise or consumption of food. Water, however, should be consumed liberally to ensure that the individual is well hydrated before the blood draw. The blood is drawn in a sterile procedure from a vein on the inner surface of the arm, in close proximity to the elbow. The entire procedure requires only a couple of minutes. Once the blood sample is procured, it is prepared for laboratory analysis.

Results from a blood test are usually available within a week. They are presented along with a normal value or range for each of the measurements. Both normal ranges and measured values can vary slightly from one laboratory to another, but the values should be fairly consistent no matter where the sample is analyzed. When you are assessing your results, keep in mind that the normal ranges are developed based on blood samples from thousands of healthy individuals and that trained athletes may differ in some respects from healthy but untrained people. The following section reviews the tests commonly performed to evaluate an athlete's health. Whenever possible, the effects of exercise training on measured levels are presented.

Stress and Immune Responses

Stressors including allergens, viruses, bacteria, and physical work can elicit responses by the immune system. While minor reactions to physical and emotional stress are normal, extreme fluctuations in immune system status can indicate problems such as illness and overtraining. A variety of markers are used to monitor immune system function.

White blood cells (WBCs). The standard composition of the five cell types that comprise white blood cells is as follows: neutrophils (62 percent), eosinophils (2.3 percent), basophils (0.4 percent), monocytes (5.3 percent), and lymphocytes (30 percent). These levels are typical, but the composition of WBCs can vary under certain conditions. For instance, eosinophils and lymphocytes can increase upon exposure to allergens, while neutrophils respond to tissue trauma and increase in response to exercise. Together, WBCs provide the bulk of the body's immunity by engulfing and destroying toxins, including foreign invaders such as viruses and bacteria, and allergens such as pollen and mold. Injuries and exercise stress severe enough to produce muscle damage also elicit a response from WBCs, as they devour damaged muscle tissue and the waste products that result from the decomposition of dead tissue.

Platelets (PLAT). Platelets are small cells produced by the bone marrow and stored in the lungs and spleen. Their primary roles are to promote blood coagulation and to secrete a growth factor that helps repair damaged blood vessels. Heavy exercise can result in a transient increase in platelet numbers.

Creatine phosphokinase (CPK or CK). Creatine phosphokinase catalyzes the reactions that form and break down creatine phosphate. Creatine phosphate, a compound used to maintain levels of the energy-supplying compound ATP, is found in abundance (along with CPK) in the heart, brain, and skeletal muscle. When the tissue from any of these is ruptured, CPK leaks into the blood. Because of its prevalence in cardiac tissue, a high blood level of CPK can indicate damage to the heart muscle and is frequently used to diagnose heart attacks. However, heavy training undertaken by athletes damages skeletal muscle, which also results in high blood levels of CPK. In fact, it is not unusual for athletes tested at the Olympic Training Center to have CPK levels ten to twelve times higher than normal levels for healthy individuals. Thus, high CPK levels may cause unnecessary concern among medical professionals if they are not aware of your athletic lifestyle.

Myoglobin (MG). A small protein molecule found in the heart and skeletal muscle, MG is similar to hemoglobin in that it has an attraction to oxygen. This attraction is responsible for the transfer of oxygen from blood to muscle tissue, where the oxygen can be used to liberate energy. As with CPK, high blood levels of MG are indicative of muscle damage.

Biochemistry Profile

These assays measure the levels of a variety of minerals, electrolytes, and other metabolites. Because of the number of variables that can affect the values of a biochemistry profile, a single reading that is out of the normal range is not always indicative of a problem. However, if a particular value is consistently high or low, an athlete may want to pursue more specific tests to investigate a possible problem.

Cholesterol (CHOL). Cholesterol belongs to a class of compounds known as monatomic alcohols and has several physiological roles. It is necessary for the formation of steroid hormones, is incorporated into cell membranes, and is part of an amalgam of compounds that makes our skin waterproof. Required amounts of cholesterol can be synthesized by the body or sequestered from the foods we eat.

Cholesterol has received much attention because of its role in the development of atherosclerosis and heart disease. These problems arise with the packaging of fats in the liver and their transport to storage sites in the adipose tissue. Fats consumed in the diet are absorbed from the intestine and transported to the liver, where they combine with cholesterol, phospholipids, and protein into a compound known as a *lipoprotein*. Lipoproteins are classified based on the amount of fat they contain, the most common classes being very low density lipoprotein (VLDL), low-density lipoprotein (LDL), and high-density lipoprotein (HDL). Because fat has the lowest density of all of a lipoprotein's components, the density of a lipoprotein decreases as its fat content increases. Thus the VLDL contains the greatest amount of fat and the HDL the least. After being synthesized by the liver, lipoproteins are released into the bloodstream. The vast majority are of the VLDL variety and are heavily loaded with fats. Upon migrating to the adipose tissue, the VLDL releases a large portion of its fat supply to the storage site in the fat tissue. This increases the density of the lipoprotein, leading to its reclassification as an LDL or HDL, depending on how much fat remains. The lipoprotein then makes its way back to the liver, where its remaining constituents can be recycled to form new lipoproteins.

High blood levels of lipoproteins, and thus cholesterol, can result in the deposition of lipoproteins in the arteries. These deposits eventually harden, leading to atherosclerosis, a disease that is responsible for nearly half of all deaths in the United States and Europe. Even more closely linked with atherosclerosis is the ratio of LDL to HDL: individuals with higher amounts of LDL in comparison to HDL are more susceptible to this disease.

A number of factors can affect lipoprotein levels. Exercise and consumption of a low-fat diet tend to have a lowering effect, while high-fat, high-calorie diets and steroid use can markedly increase blood lipoprotein levels.

Protein. The blood contains a wide variety of proteins responsible for a range of tasks. The two most abundant blood proteins are albumin (ALB) and globulin (GLOB). Collectively, blood proteins help to maintain plasma volume and pH balance and provide a reserve of amino acids that can supply energy to the working muscle or repair muscle tissue following a workout. Other proteins transport hormones, growth factors, and vitamins to their target tissues. Note that these protein parameters do not reflect dietary protein need and should not be used to guide protein consumption.

Calcium (Ca). The most abundant mineral in the human body, calcium , with phosphorus, forms the hard material that makes up bones and teeth. It is also involved in metabolic processes such as muscle contraction, nerve impulse conduction, blood clotting, and the maintenance of acid-base balance in the blood. Low circulating levels of calcium prompt the release of parathyroid hormone, which mobilizes calcium from bone. When circulating levels are high, the excess calcium is either excreted or used to maintain bone density.

Phosphorus (INP or P_i). Phosphorus joins with calcium to provide the structure of bone. Phosphate also is involved with blood acid-base balance and is a vital ingredient of the high-energy compounds ATP and creatine phosphate.

Magnesium (Mg). While not as plentiful as calcium or phosphorus, magnesium is essential for a number of physiological reactions, especially those involved with carbohydrate metabolism. Magnesium also acts in opposition to calcium in the muscle contraction-relaxation cycle: calcium is required for a muscle to contract, magnesium for it to relax. Thus, a magnesium deficiency can result in muscle spasms and cramps.

Sodium (Na), potassium (K), and chloride (Cl). These three minerals are commonly known as *electrolytes*. Collectively, they are important for the transmission of nerve impulses and contractility of the heart and skeletal muscles. Because they promote fluid retention, they are heavily involved in maintaining hydration. During periods of dehydration, the body retains great amounts of these minerals until hydration is restored.

Waste Products

Some by-products of normal cellular metabolism are either partially salvaged or excreted by the body. The biochemistry profile typically screens for the following by-products.

Ammonia (AMMON). Ammonia is a nitrogen-containing by-product of protein catabolism (breakdown). Increased blood levels can be seen with high-protein diets but also can indicate muscle damage or an increase in the use of protein as an energy source. Athletes who consume low-carbohydrate diets or perform endurance exercise with depleted glycogen stores rely more heavily on protein as an energy source and typically have elevated blood ammonia levels.

Blood urea nitrogen (BUN). When ammonia is combined with carbon dioxide, urea is produced. Filtration of urea through the kidneys is the primary mode for eliminating nitrogen from the body. In cases of kidney damage, the rate of urea filtration may be compromised, leading to an elevation of blood urea nitrogen.

Creatinine (CREA). This metabolite results from the breakdown of creatine. Creatinine is filtered by the kidney and eliminated through the urine. In sedentary individuals, creatinine levels are fairly constant from day to day and high blood creatinine suggests abnormal kidney function. However, heavy exercise may cause sufficient damage to muscle fibers to cause creatinine to leak into the blood. Creatine supplementation, a common practice among some athletes (see chapter 10), may also increase blood creatinine levels. Therefore, high blood creatinine levels in athletes don't necessarily indicate kidney problems.

Uric acid (URIC). Uric acid results from the breakdown of purines, a family of molecules that provides the backbone for DNA and RNA. Adenosine, the core molecule of ATP, is also a purine. Clinically, high levels of uric acids are indicative of gout, a painful, arthritic joint condition. However, purine levels can also rise following heavy exercise or as a result of a high-protein diet or amino acid supplementation.

Enzymes

Enzymes are protein molecules that catalyze (speed up) chemical reactions. Thousands of enzymes in the human body, each catalyzing one specific reaction, are involved with processes such as digestion, energy liberation, and transcription (the reproduction of DNA). Many enzymes increase in response to training. A biochemistry profile typically tracks enzymes whose abnormal levels indicate a pathological condition or illness.

Alkaline phosphatase (ALK). Alkaline phosphatase is found in white blood cells and a variety of organs and tissues including the liver, kidneys, and adrenal glands and high blood levels can indicate damage or disease in these organs and tissues. However, the greatest concentration of ALK is in bone, as this enzyme helps catalyze the deposition of calcium into the bone. Thus, blood levels of ALK can reflect the rate of bone formation. Because adolescents form bone more rapidly than adults, they typically have higher ALK levels. The use of antibiotics and oral contraceptives can also cause ALK to rise.

Lactate dehydrogenase (LDH). This enzyme is involved in the production and metabolism of lactic acid. Interestingly, lactate dehydrogenase exists in two subforms: LDHc, which predominates in cardiac muscle, and LDHm, which is more plentiful in skeletal muscle. LDHm catalyzes the formation of lactic acid from pyruvic acid at the end of glycolysis, while LDHc catalyzes the reverse reaction that converts lactic acid back into pyruvic acid. Aerobically trained muscle has a great capacity to consume pyruvic acid via the aerobic energy pathway, so the presence of the LDHc isoform allows muscle tissue to recycle lactate by converting it into a usable energy substrate (pyruvate). The heart muscle is perhaps the most aerobically trained muscle in the body (consider that the only time it can rest is between heartbeats!); thus high levels of LDHc in the cardiac muscle help supply adequate amounts of pyruvate. As you may suspect, aerobic training increases the amount of the LDHc isoform in skeletal muscle. This is because the increased aerobic capacity of trained muscle increases its ability to consume pyruvic acid.

As with other enzymes that are confined to the muscle tissue, elevated levels of LDH in the blood indicate tissue damage. By differentiating between LDHc and LDHm, technicians can better isolate the damage. High blood levels of LDHm or a mixture of LDHm and LDHc indicate damage to skeletal muscle, while high levels of LDHc indicate damage to cardiac tissue, often suggesting a heart attack.

Serum glutamine oxaloacetic transaminase (SGOT) and serum glutamate pyruvate transaminase (SGPT). These enzymes are involved with the metabolism of the amino acid glutamine. They are abundant in the liver, skeletal muscle, and heart (SGOT only). Damage to any of these organs will result in elevated levels of SGPT and/or SGOT. SGOT may also be elevated in cases of infectious mononucleosis. As with CPK and LDH, heavy training loads can result in abnormally high levels of SGOT and SGPT.

Complete Blood Count (CBC) and Iron Profile

These tests measure the various constituents of the blood's oxygen transport system. Red blood cells are responsible for transporting oxygen in the bloodstream, but other constituents within the CBC and iron profile, such as hemoglobin, haptoglobin, ferretin, and iron, play important roles in the formation and function of the red blood cells. Because oxygen delivery to working muscle is vital to the success of endurance cyclists, these values should be monitored to ensure that all aspects of this system are working properly.

Hematocrit (HCT). Hematocrit, the total of all solid material in the blood, consists primarily of red blood cells. Since these cells transport oxygen throughout the body, hematocrit levels are often used as a measure of the oxygen-carrying capacity of the blood.

Hemoglobin (HG). Hemoglobin is a large, iron-containing molecule located in the red blood cell. The iron atom within hemoglobin attracts an oxygen molecule, giving the red blood cell its oxygen-carrying ability.

Mean corpuscular hemoglobin (MCH). Mean corpuscular hemoglobin is a measure of the amount of hemoglobin in the average red blood cell.

Mean corpuscular volume (MCV). Mean corpuscular volume is a measure of the size of red blood cells. Young red blood cells tend to be larger than older cells, so a high value indicates recent production of cells by the bone marrow, while a low value indicates a small population of young red cells and a possible drop in red blood cell production. Thus, evaluation of MCV can help determine the effectiveness of altitude training in stimulating red blood cell production or can be used as one of several markers of anemia.

Reticulocytes (RETIC). Reticulocytes are immature red blood cells. Like MCV, RETIC levels can be used to assess how recently red blood cells were produced. High numbers indicate recent production, whereas low numbers can indicate iron deficiency, because the body cannot produce red blood cells without iron. Monitoring RETIC counts is often used to evaluate the effectiveness of iron supplementation in anemic individuals.

Haptoglobin (HPT). Haptoglobin is a large protein molecule that attaches to free hemoglobin in the blood. When red blood cells are destroyed, hemoglobin is released, bound by haptoglobin, and transported to the bone marrow, where it can be incorporated into newly synthesized red blood cells. A test for HPT measures only the haptoglobin that is not bound to hemoglobin. Thus, low HPT levels can indicate an increased rate of destruction of red blood cells.

Total bilirubin (TBIL). When aged red blood cells are destroyed, a small portion of the hemoglobin is converted into bilirubin. Bilirubin is always present at low levels in the blood, as older red blood cells are constantly being destroyed and their contents recycled. Bilirubin is processed in the liver, and total bilirubin levels are often used to indicate liver disease. In athletes, high bilirubin levels can indicate a predisposition to anemia, as they can result from an increase in red cell destruction and a decrease in the salvaging of hemoglobin used for the production of new red blood cells.

Iron (Fe). A heavy metal found in hemoglobin, iron has a remarkable affinity for oxygen; by binding oxygen molecules, it allows red blood cells to carry oxygen from the lungs to the working muscle and other tissues. Low levels of iron in the blood can indicate iron deficiency and a reduced capacity to transport oxygen.

Ferritin (FERR). When red blood cells are destroyed, iron is released into the blood and bound by a protein called transferrin to form a complex called ferritin. FERR deposits the iron in the bone marrow, where it is used in the production of new red blood cells. Low ferritin levels can indicate a reduced ability to salvage iron, leading to iron deficiency.

Total iron-binding capacity (TIBC). Transferrin is quantified by its capacity to bind iron. Normally, transferrin has about one third of its binding sites occupied by iron. High total iron-binding capacity levels indicate that the body is mobilizing large amounts of iron. Low TIBC levels are often indicative of an inflammatory response.

Percent saturation (SAT). Percent saturation, the ratio of blood iron concentration to TIBC level, is usually about 20 to 40 percent. Low SAT values can indicate inhibited iron transport ability, possibly due to low iron stores.

Blood Tests and Iron Deficiency Anemia

Anemia, a reduction in red blood cells and/or hemoglobin, causes symptoms including fatigue, headache, and pallor. Athletes with anemia will almost certainly notice a decrease in their ability to perform work due to the reduced oxygen-carrying capacity of the blood. The most common cause of anemia is inadequate bodily stores of iron brought on by insufficient dietary consumption and/or poor absorption of dietary iron. Vegetarian athletes and those who are on calorie-restricted diets are particularly at risk. Among these groups, menstruating women are at an even higher risk, as significant amounts of iron can be lost as a result of menstrual bleeding.

A diet deficient in vitamin B12 and/or folic acid may also predispose an individual to anemia. A shortage of these nutrients can lead to the formation of red blood cells that are fragile, malformed, susceptible to rupture, and short-lived. The short life of these red blood cells necessitates a higher rate of red blood cell production, which may exhaust iron stores and lead to anemia.

Anemia is diagnosed based on evaluations of blood levels of iron, iron-binding capacity, and percent saturation in association with hemoglobin levels. Typically, an abnormal test result for any one of these markers does not signal anemia, but a pattern of abnormal results as well as other ostensive symptoms are used to make a diagnosis. The guidelines shown in the table on the next page can be used to help diagnose true anemia.

It is important to note that a single test that places an athlete in stage 1 or 2 does not necessarily mean the athlete is at risk for anemia or will see a decrease in exercise performance. Nevertheless, these athletes should be monitored with follow-up tests to determine if their iron status is deteriorating. Furthermore, athletes in stage 1 or 2 may want to assess their dietary intake for iron and should be alert to the overt symptoms of anemia.

Prevention and Treatment of Iron Deficiency Anemia

Proper dietary intake of iron is the best way to prevent iron deficiency anemia. Men should strive to consume at least 10 to 12 milligrams

ANEMIA DIAGNOSIS GUIDELINES

	FERRITIN (g/dL)	PERCENT SATURATION	HEMOGLOBIN (g/dL)
NORMAL	≥12	›16	›12
STAGE 1 (DEPLETION OF STORAGE IRON)	‹12	›16	›12
STAGE 2 (DECREASED TRANSPORT IRON)	‹12	‹16	›12
STAGE 3 (IRON DEFICIENCY ANEMIA)	‹12	‹16	‹12

of iron per day, while women should consume at least 18 to 20 milligrams. The following dietary strategies can help to ensure proper iron consumption.

- eat more red meat or dark meat from poultry
- consume vitamin C with meals to improve iron absorption
- cook meals in a cast-iron skillet on a regular basis
- consume a multivitamin-mineral supplement containing iron daily (if prone to iron deficiency anemia, try a supplement with 325 milligrams of ferrous sulfate three times per week; note that the ferrous form of iron, with the exception of ferrous fumarate, is easily absorbed but the ferric form is not, so look for iron supplements with ferrous iron salts such as ferrous sulfate or ferrous gluconate)

In addition to these tips, be aware that certain foods can inhibit iron absorption from the intestine. If you consume calcium, phosphate, bran, polyphenols (found in teas), or antacids, you may want to space your intake so as not to consume iron supplements or iron-rich foods at the same time.

Treatment of iron deficiency anemia should include a reduction in training workload and iron supplementation with 100 milligrams of ferrous sulfate per day for one to three months. Monthly blood tests should be performed during treatment to monitor its success. Improvements in ferritin, mean corpuscular volume, percent saturation, and hemoglobin levels, along with the appearance of significant numbers of reticulocytes, are positive signs that the supplementation strategy is working.

Finally, a warning: True anemia among endurance athletes is not common. While many athletes may exhibit certain blood markers of anemia, the rate of true anemia among athletes is in the range of 3 to 5 percent. The reason for this discrepancy is that regular aerobic exercise increases plasma volume and can dilute red blood cell and hemoglobin concentrations to anemic levels. This condition, known as *sports anemia* or *false anemia,* is benign and does not reflect low iron stores or inhibit exercise performance. Care should be taken to arrive at a proper diagnosis, as significant iron supplementation in athletes with sports anemia does nothing to improve performance and is wasteful and potentially dangerous. Large dosages of iron can inhibit absorption of antibiotics and minerals such as zinc and copper, and high blood iron levels have been associated with heart attacks, cancer, and the development of diabetes. Thus, evaluation of iron status and treatment of iron deficiency anemia should be monitored by a doctor or hematologist.

Questions and Answers

Q. The local sports medicine clinic provides lactate threshold tests but does so by collecting and analyzing my expired air. Is this an accurate method of determining lactate threshold?
A. The clinic is actually determining *ventilatory threshold,* which usually occurs near the same exercise intensity as lactate threshold. If you are willing to incur the expense and inconvenience of professional testing, you should seek a facility that will draw blood and actually measure blood lactate levels. Otherwise, you can probably get similarly accurate results using a power meter and testing yourself at home.

Q. Do road cyclists really need to do Wingate tests?
A. For most road cyclists the answer is no. The Wingate test is most helpful for track sprinters who rely heavily on short-term explosive power.

Q. I am a male cyclist who undergoes routine blood tests. My hematocrit is typically in the low 40s. A friend of mine, also a guy, usually has a hematocrit in the high 40s or even the low 50s. Why are we so different?
A. This is likely due to a natural variability in hematocrit levels. When blood oxygen levels are low, the body produces erythropoietin, the hormone that stimulates red blood cell production. Genetic differences that affect sensitivity to low blood oxygen levels and the activity of the gene that produces erythropoietin can produce wide variations in individual hematocrit levels. Just to be on the safe side, check your ferritin, percent saturation, and hemoglobin levels to guard against anemia.

Part Two

TRAINING
PLANS

Kimberly Bruckner solos to her first national road championship. Well-planned and well-executed training programs are important to success in competitive cycling.

CHAPTER 4

Training Philosophies

Now that we have reviewed the basic foundations of physiology and metabolism, it's time to apply this knowledge to designing training programs. First of all, what is training? There are a number of definitions, but for our purposes training can be defined as a systematic regimen that alternates periods of physical stress with rest and recovery to improve an athlete's ability to perform work. A training program is a detailed, well thought out, long-term training schedule for an individual. To properly design and implement a training program, athletes and coaches should bear in mind the following concepts, which provide a foundation for understanding how the body responds to exercise stress.

Overload. This concept refers to taxing the body with a physiological stress greater than that which the body routinely experiences.

Supercompensation. When the body is subjected to overload, it undergoes physiological changes that improve its ability to perform work. The result of supercompensation is known as a *training effect.*

When faced with resistance training, for example, the body responds by building more muscle tissue, leading to an increase in strength. Aerobic exercise and high-intensity intervals lead to increases in numbers of mitochondria, in enzymes that catalyze reactions of the energy pathways, in the number of capillaries that supply blood to the working muscles, and even in blood volume. All of these responses increase the rate at which energy can be supplied to the working muscle.

Progressive overload. This concept refers to the use of escalating training loads over time to elicit continued supercompensation and a progressively greater training effect.

Because the body can supercompensate, it requires progressively greater overload to improve its ability to perform work. Consider a cyclist who sets an off-season goal of increasing leg strength. To do so, the rider begins by performing a set of eight back squats with a weight of 200 pounds. At first, this task is somewhat difficult, as the athlete is not accustomed to this type of overload. However, because of the body's ability to supercompensate, the rider's lower body strength eventually increases to the point that doing a set of eight squats at 200 pounds becomes relatively easy. At this point, supercompensation for this task is complete and strength gains will plateau unless the amount of weight lifted (overload) is increased beyond 200 pounds.

Specific overload leads to a specific response. The body will adapt to a specific overload with a specific response.

Let's return to the above example of the cyclist who is trying to increase leg strength. The rider can expect the squats regimen to improve leg strength, but would not expect an increase in arm and shoulder strength, because the exercise places load specifically on the trunk and legs.

The concept of specific adaptation applies to practically every training task. For instance, sprint training has little effect on aerobic endurance capacity, as sprinting primarily taxes the anaerobic system. Likewise, high-volume, low-intensity training may do wonders to improve aerobic conditioning but can actually diminish a rider's sprinting ability.

Specificity of training. This concept refers to the degree of similarity between training tasks and the requirements of competition. A general goal when designing a training program is to develop workouts with tasks similar to those found in competition. In other words, train like you race. Consider match-sprinters who rely on muscular power to create the speed and explosiveness needed for an event that typically lasts from eight to ten seconds. Endurance (the ability to race for several hours) is not an issue for the match-sprinter; thus, training for this event should focus primarily on short, high-intensity efforts rather than long, low-intensity rides. At the other extreme are athletes who compete in ultra-endurance events like the Race across America. Sprinting ability is of little consequence to the outcome of such races, so short, high-intensity sprints are less useful in training for them.

Although training specificity is an important concept to keep in mind when designing training programs, there are exceptions to this rule. For instance, although weight training has little in common with pedaling a bicycle, a properly designed resistance program can be useful in improving performance in cycling competitions of all lengths.

Individual response. Everyone differs in their ability to respond to training. While a given training stimulus will elicit the same type of training response in all individuals, the magnitude of that response will vary from one athlete to another because of their differing genetic makeups. Thus, two athletes can follow the same training program and respond quite differently. It has been said that the single best thing an individual can do in the quest to become a champion is to choose the right parents. There appears to be a great deal of truth to this statement, as while champions are not born, the ability to become a champion is inborn. However, do not think that a superior genetic makeup guarantees the success of an athlete. Genetics gives individuals their potential, but hard work, determination, and good choices make them champions.

Assessing Current Abilities

Now that you have a handle on the basics of exercise physiology and the concepts of training, it's time to develop a training plan. But before you start marking races on the calendar and devising workouts, you need to take an inventory of yourself. Evaluating who you are and where you want to go in the sport will give you a sense of direction, which is necessary for formulating a plan. The process of self-evaluation should include:

current physical conditioning
- maximal oxygen consumption
- lactate threshold/maximal steady state
- strengths: what do I do well?
- weaknesses: where do I need to improve?

psychological status
- what do I want to ultimately achieve?

- what am I prepared to do to achieve my goals?
  - how much time am I willing or able to devote to training and racing?
  - how much money am I willing or able to spend?
  - how much pain am I willing to endure?
  - how motivated am I?
- **lifestyle issues**
  - family responsibilities
  - job or career responsibilities

Setting Goals

Setting proper goals is one of the most important, yet often overlooked, aspects of developing a training plan. Its importance cannot be overemphasized; after all, the first step in getting somewhere is knowing where you are going. Established goals provide a sense of direction and focus, while a desire to reach goals set in advance of a training program provides motivation to train and improve. And finally, reaching goals provides satisfaction and a sense of accomplishment, which leads to greater motivation.

Because of their importance, goals should be carefully planned and contemplated. So when you take the time to set meaningful goals, consider the following.

Dream

Before setting goals, allow yourself to dream about where you want to go in cycling. Dream about the greatest objective you could hope to accomplish. This is not the time to limit yourself with reality, so dream big. What would you like to accomplish if you were able to overcome all obstacles? Set this dream as your highest target for which to aim. The likelihood of achieving this dream may be infinitesimally small, but that's fine. Even if you never realize your dream, aiming high will allow you to view yourself as being without limits and to break through barriers that may otherwise seem unconquerable.

Set Long-, Intermediate-, and Short-Term Goals

Long-term goals focus on the "big picture," and you should strive to achieve them within two to five years. While long-term goals should be somewhat more realistic than your dream, they should still stretch your limits. Challenge yourself by seeking accomplishments that presently seem to be just outside of your potential. For a junior rider, a good long-term goal may be to race as a professional. A masters athlete may want to finish in the top twenty at the Masters' World Championship. Whatever the long-term goal, establish it and set a realistic timetable for achieving it. Be aware, however, that events may compel you to change your long-term goals. For instance, a talented young rider new to the sport may quickly eclipse the long-term goals she or he set just a few months earlier. This rider would require a new set of long-term goals on which to focus. Thus, build some degree of flexibility into your long-term plans, as both the time frames for accomplishing these goals and the goals themselves may require occasional adjustments.

Intermediate-term goals, with a time horizon of one to two years, require significantly more thought than long-term goals because they are much more specific. Intermediate-term goals need to be reasonable and measurable, and the ability to attain them should be almost entirely under your control. Not following these three guidelines can lead to goals that may be impossible to achieve. For instance, before taking on a new client, I always ask them what they want to achieve in the next two years. Often they tell me they want to win a particular race, sometimes even that they want

Not all situations can be foreseen or controlled. These riders are recovering from an unexpected crash and are out of contention in this race.

to win it next year. This desire is inappropriate as an intermediate-term goal, as there are too many variables associated with winning a particular race that are totally out of a person's control. Bad weather, illness, and mechanical problems are just a few of the pitfalls that can keep an otherwise prepared rider from winning a race, even if she or he is the strongest rider in the competition. Also out of a person's control is the nature of the competition. Performance in a mass-start race depends not only on how well you and your teammates are riding, but also on how well the competition is performing. Thus, winning the race or improving your competitive placement compared to the previous year may not provide an accurate measurement of your progress as an athlete. More appropriate choices for intermediate-term goals might

be increasing your MSPO by 10 percent or improving your time in a weekly club time trial by 5 percent over the previous year.

Short-term goals range in time from the immediate to several months in the future. Setting up a training plan by determining which races to ride, the volume and intensity of workouts, and the progression of the training plan toward intermediate- and long-term goals are all examples of short-term goals. When setting short-term goals, follow these guidelines:

- they should be specific, quantifiable, and attainable
- they should contribute to the accomplishment of intermediate- and long-term goals
- they should be flexible enough to accommodate changing circumstances

It is very important that short-term goals be specific, quantifiable, and attainable. With specific and quantifiable goals, an athlete has a clear plan to follow. For instance, setting the goal of doing a hard interval workout leaves an athlete with little sense of direction and may result in a workout that does not provide the proper training stress. A more useful goal would be to specify the number, duration, and intensity of the work intervals as well as the duration of the rest intervals in a workout. Prescribing a workout of six, five-minute intervals at 300 watts separated by two minutes of rest not only provides the athlete with specific goals that can be clearly met, but it also can be more easily integrated into a long-term training plan by providing the rider with a specific training stress.

Short-term goals should also be difficult to achieve, but ultimately attainable. No one likes to fail, and most athletes who consistently fail to meet their goals will eventually lose their motivation to train and compete. Furthermore, athletes who frequently fail to meet their goals run the risk of becoming motivated by a fear of failure. While this can provide motivation, it should not be a primary motivator because it can lead an athlete to do not his or her absolute best, but only enough to avoid failing. Secondly, failure does little to build self-confidence, and athletes who lack self-confidence seldom push their own limits. So, when setting your short-term goals, be sure they are demanding but realistic, for having short-term goals that are beyond your reach sets you up for consistent failure and discouragement. Reaching goals that are difficult but not impossible will provide you with a sense of accomplishment and lead to a positive outlook and greater motivation to succeed.

Short-term goals must also contribute to the accomplishment of intermediate- and long-term goals. A training plan is not unlike the blueprints for a building, with the long-term goal forming a single, solid, functional structure and the short-term goals providing the bricks used to build that structure. Each relatively tiny brick must be laid precisely and in proper order to achieve the long-term goal of building a massive skyscraper.

Thus, when setting your short-term goals, be aware of their purpose in the pursuit of your longer-term goals. For a fine example of this, witness the Tour of Italy. While the Giro itself is a very demanding race and quite an accomplishment to win, many participants have the bigger goal of winning or placing high in the Tour de France a month later. These competitors who use the Giro solely to train for the Tour de France often finish well toward the bottom in Italy. However, the fitness they gain by racing the Giro helps them be competitive in France. So, these riders can successfully meet their goals for the Tour of Italy in spite of their poor placings. This perspective should be extended to your workouts as well: each day of your training program should have a particular purpose, whether it is to complete a six-hour ride or to stay off the bike and recover. Recognize each workout or competition both for its short-term purpose and for its role in the scheme of your intermediate- and long-term goals.

Assessing current circumstances when setting and evaluating short-term goals means being aware of external and internal factors that can affect performance. External factors such as mechanical failures and poor weather conditions can be uncontrollable and have a dramatic effect on an athlete's competitive placement. I recall a time trial stage during the Tour de France a few years ago that illustrates this point quite well. Early in the day, when the slower riders were on the course, weather conditions were pleasant and the riders enjoyed a slight tailwind. As the day wore on, a cold

Charley Mottet discusses strategy with his teammates before the Montreal World Cup. Although only one person can win the event, each rider can have a successful race by contributing to the success of his team.

front passed through the area and the weather conditions changed drastically. Toward the end of the day's competition, the higher-placed riders were competing in heavy rain and riding into a strong headwind. Although the times for the riders who raced later in the day suggested that they performed poorly, it was clear that it was not the abilities of the riders but the weather that had the greatest influence on performance that day.

Internal factors can also have a profound effect on training goals and performance. For instance, a rider afflicted with a common cold or the flu may find it all but impossible to complete a strenuous workout. Too often in these situations, athletes struggle to do their workouts but are unable to complete them because of their illness. Furthermore, they often compound the problem by having negative feelings about falling

short of the prescribed workout. A better approach would be to recognize that having an illness may necessitate a change in short-term goals and that the best objective for the day may be to rest and return to good health. This strategy allows the rider not only to speed her return to serious training, but also to feel confident that she did the best thing she could do on that day.

Achieving the Most Important Goal

Each long-, intermediate-, and short-term goal plays a role in the development of a training program. Some may seem less important than others; some may be easy to achieve, while others may be quite difficult. However, there is one goal that should be the most important goal of every athlete, regardless of age, ability, gender, or situation. This goal is remarkably simple to set, yet challenging to achieve. It is not winning a particular race, making an Olympic team, or signing a pro contract. The most important goal of all is to simply do your absolute best in any given situation.

As simple as this may sound, it is probably the most overlooked and underachieved goal in the history of mankind. One of the biggest mistakes made by people from all walks of life is neglecting to make the most out of the present. Athletes are no exception, as many fail to realize that success requires not only a complete commitment to the future, but also a complete commitment to the present. This is because although you can plan and work toward attaining goals set in the future, the only time frame you can truly control is right now, and you only have one chance to make the most of it. Life is the ul-

timate game, played with no time-outs, no free laps, and no do-overs, and getting the most out of yourself in the future means always demanding nothing less than the best from yourself in the present.

An excellent example of what it means to make the most out of the present is something I see frequently when reviewing the SRM files from clients' workouts. If I prescribe ten intervals for a particular workout, often the power output will be significantly higher on the tenth and final interval than on the previous nine. When I ask clients why this is the case, they usually respond by saying that because it was the final interval, they wanted to make the most of it. When I point out that they had nine other chances to make the most of it and failed to take advantage of the opportunities, they begin to understand what I mean by always making the most out of the present.

Mari Holden pouring on the power.

CHAPTER 5

Formulating a Training Schedule

Success in road racing and mountain bike competition depends on three basic physiological ingredients: endurance, sustainable power, and nonsustainable power. The proper combination of these three components makes the cyclist a well-rounded competitor, and each should be developed to a degree that meets the competitive needs of the rider. For instance, a rider who primarily competes in criteriums would place far more emphasis on short, nonsustainable power than a cyclist focusing on stage racing or time trialing. Thus, your competitive goals have a bearing on your approach to training.

Since I began working for the USOC in 1992, I have been involved in testing hundreds of cyclists of varying abilities, and I've learned that the physiological variable that most separates elite road cyclists from their subelite counterparts is MSPO. While maximal oxygen consumption, lactate threshold, exercising heart rate, and riding economy values are very similar between the two groups, elite cyclists set themselves apart by being able to produce and sustain higher power outputs than subelite riders.

MSPO stands alone as the most reliable physiological predictor of success among road cyclists. After all, the winner of the race is the person who can complete the required distance in the shortest time. While drafting, teamwork, and positioning play some role in determining the first to finish, the person who can pedal at the highest power output and thus maintain the highest speed holds a definite advantage. In time trials, the ability to produce more power creates an even greater advantage; no drafting is allowed, so the fastest rider will win the event.

Possibly the greatest testament to the importance of building a high MSPO is 2000 Olympic Silver Medalist and World Champion Mari Holden. I first met Mari in 1993 when I was working as a physiologist at the U.S. Olympic Training Center in Colorado Springs. By this time, Mari was already recognized as one of the finest triathletes in the country. However, on this occasion, she was participating in a cycling camp put on by then National Cycling Team coach Henny Top. While being tested in our lab, Mari produced one of the highest VO_2 max levels I've ever seen for a female athlete. Despite her exceptionally high VO_2 max, however, Mari's MSPO was far below average for elite women cyclists. It was obvious that her power output would have to increase if she were to ever reach her enormous potential. Mari's race outcomes reflected her laboratory results—at times she was competitive, but her performances were well below those of the top riders and fell short of her potential.

Not long after testing Mari, I began my doctoral studies at Ohio State University in the autumn of 1993. In early 1994, the U.S. Cycling Federation hired Dean Golich as a physiologist, and he also noticed Mari's potential and recognized the need to increase her power output. Dean's approach to training was somewhat novel at the time, placing great emphasis on weight training and high-intensity intervals. Dean also experimented with a relatively new approach to training in which athletes perform their intervals on two to three consecutive days. This type of training, which I refer to as *block training,* alternates several days of very hard training with several days of rest and will be covered in greater detail in chapter 6. Dean's training strategy proved successful: within eighteen months, Mari's MSPO had increased by 60 watts and she won her first of five national time trial titles. Mari also went on to win a silver medal in the time trial at the 2000 Olympic Games and was the world champion in the event in 2000.

So how can you increase MSPO? A high MSPO depends on two basic components: a well-developed cardiovascular system that can deliver oxygen and other nutrients to the working muscle and a highly refined muscular system that can use the oxygen and energy substrates to produce power. Most cyclists are adept at developing the cardiovascular system. Lots of riding and a moderate amount of high-intensity intervals will sufficiently strengthen the heart muscle, increase the vascularity of the muscle tissue, increase blood volume, and improve the oxygen-carrying capacity of the blood. However, developing the muscular system takes time and several phases of training.

Compared to cardiovascular conditioning, it is a complicated process that is not well understood by many competitive cyclists.

The cardiovascular system can be trained to transport large amounts of oxygen and energy substrates. However, the working muscle must be properly trained before it can fully utilize these nutrients. Well-trained muscle fibers can consume more oxygen and produce more power than untrained muscles and are vital to the exercising athlete. Recall from chapter 1 that different types of muscle fibers have different twitch characteristics. Some fibers possess great endurance but have little power, some produce powerful contractions but lack endurance, and many others exist somewhere in between these two extremes. Until recently, it was believed that each person's muscle fiber composition was determined genetically. In other words, you are born with a predetermined amount of each type of fiber and nothing can change this composition. However, a growing body of evidence suggests that training can influence the twitch characteristics of muscle fibers.

Thus, a properly designed training program should include specialized workouts that build muscle tissue, paying particular attention to strengthening slower-twitch muscle fibers and improving the aerobic capacity of faster-twitch fibers without compromising their power. The training approach presented in chapters 7 and 8 results in muscle tissue that not only can produce a lot of power, but can maintain that power for extended periods, resulting in a higher MSPO.

Prescribing and Monitoring Workout Intensity

Proper workout intensity is necessary to realize benefits from training. After all, your success in bicycle racing is largely determined by your ability to work at a faster rate than your competitors. So monitoring exercise intensity is an important aspect of any training program. Heart rate and power output are the two most common gauges of workout intensity. While heart rate monitors have been used extensively by athletes over the past fifteen years, devices designed to measure power output are relatively new. Regardless of the method you use, understanding how to use the device *and* the data obtained from it is the first step in improving the quality of a training program.

Using a Heart Rate Monitor

Athletes, coaches, and physiologists have long recognized the relationship between work intensity and heart rate. Generally, as exercise intensity increases, so does heart rate. This established relationship has given rise to the widespread use of heart rate monitors to measure and guide exercise intensity. Many cyclists—from novice to elite—now use these devices. Workout intensities are frequently prescribed in percentages of either *maximal* or *threshold* heart rates, and many athletes use their heart rates as a tool to micromanage every workout.

While monitoring heart rate can help in guiding workout intensity and monitoring training loads, the method is not without shortcomings. A number of factors besides exercise intensity can affect exercising heart rates and confound users of these monitors. Nervousness, lack of sleep, high ambient temperatures, and dehydration can cause higher than normal heart rates during exercise, while fatigue from the previous day's workout can depress exercising heart rate. Altitude exposure exerts a dual effect on exercising heart rate; it typically increases submaximal heart rate but decreases maximal heart rate.

Athletes who utilize heart rate monitors often do not recognize that the important measurement during exercise isn't heart rate, but *work rate,* or power. I frequently tell my clients that heart rates don't win races, power outputs do, and heart rate simply offers an estimate of power output. Although data from heart rate monitors can be useful, it can also be misleading and confusing. Thus, to use a heart rate monitor effectively, one must recognize all of its shortcomings.

Another common mistake made by cyclists is failing to recognize the lag time between the start of work and the increase in heart rate. The graph on the next page shows the relationship between power output and heart rate for a cyclist performing a five-minute interval at a prescribed work rate of 375 watts. In this cyclist, this work rate typically elicits a heart rate of 168 beats per minute. However, notice that the heart rate does not reach this level until the rider has been working for approximately three minutes. This is a normal reaction, as it takes time for the body to respond to exercise and increase the heart rate. A potential problem arises when a rider who uses heart rate to prescribe workout intensity believes that his or her heart rate must be at the prescribed level of 168 beats per minute before the proper workout intensity is reached. In other words, the rider believes that the intensity for the first three minutes of the interval is too low. Of course this belief is incorrect, as the power output clearly shows that the rider is at the correct intensity for the entire interval. Nevertheless, this confusion can cause the athlete either to work excessively hard early in the interval to achieve the target heart rate more quickly or to believe that the interval does not begin until the target heart rate is reached, resulting in an overly long interval. This lag time between the start of work and the increase in heart rate is even more of a problem for shorter intervals. In fact, during intervals of one minute or less, exercise pe-

Power (watts) ———— Heart Rate (bpm) ++++++++++

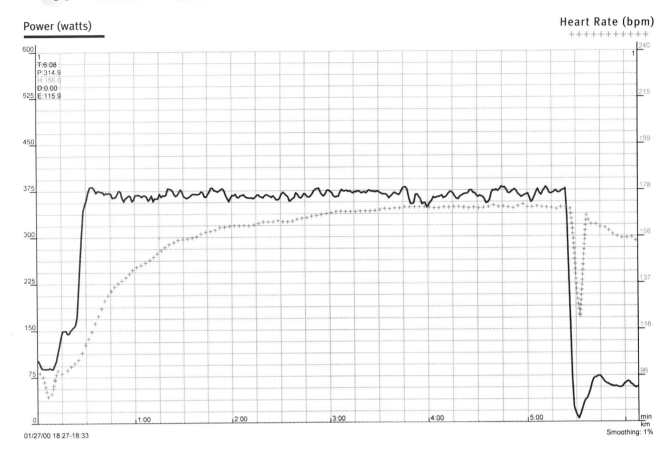

01/27/00 18:27-18:33   Smoothing: 1%

Power output and heart rate for a five-minute interval. Notice that the even though the proper power output is achieved within a few seconds, the prescribed heart rate for the interval is not reached for several minutes.

riods are so short and intensity generally so high that heart rate becomes practically useless for measuring exercise intensity.

Despite their shortcomings, heart rate monitors will continue to be popular because they are relatively inexpensive and widely available. If you do choose to use one, be aware of its limitations and make adjustments when necessary. When utilizing block training, you should employ a number of backup methods to monitor your work intensity during the second and third day of a training block. If you are doing intervals on a trainer,

try to stick with the same gear, cadence, and resistance setting that you used on the first day of your block, when your heart rate is most likely to reflect your actual power output. If you are training on the road, use landmarks to gauge your progress. Finally, learn to gauge your intensity based on how you feel. Learn how each type of interval should feel. Learn what it feels like to be working at or above threshold. Above all, while you should use the data from your heart rate monitor, don't assume that the data always accurately reflect how hard you're working.

Using Power Output to Monitor and Prescribe Intensity

When I began working for the USOC in 1992, there was a bicycle in our lab with a bicycle crank outfitted with strain gauges and interfaced to a small control box mounted to the handlebars. This setup, known as the *Powerscan,* was built by Don Witte, an engineer from Boulder, Colorado. The instrument was able to accurately measure power output, but could not store data, was heavy, and wasn't weatherproof. Thus, it was not practical to use outdoors on a racing bicycle. I can remember thinking what a useful piece of equipment this power meter could be if only it could be used in practical situations. Little did I know that at that very time, Uli Schoberer, a young German engineer, was working on just such a device. This instrument, now known as the *SRM* (for Schoberer Resistance Monitor), was being used at the U.S. Cycling Federation when I went to work there as a physiologist in 1995. With the SRM, I could measure exactly the amount of work and the intensity of effort required for a cyclist to be competitive in any given race. The data could then be used to prescribe and monitor training that more closely matched the demands of competitive events.

Today, there are a number of devices for measuring power output on a bicycle. Their primary advantage is that instead of estimating power output, as heart rate does, they actually measure work rate. To illustrate the superiority of using power output versus heart rate to prescribe and monitor training intensity, consider the following example. As stated earlier, fatigue resulting from multiple days of difficult training can decrease exercising heart rate. Many coaches and athletes believe this simply reflects a body that is too tired to maintain work levels over several consecutive days

of training. As a result, many athletes are reluctant to do high-intensity intervals on successive days. However, data collected with the SRM clearly show this line of thinking to be incorrect. The graph on the next page illustrates the data from a cyclist who performed three-minute intervals at 350 watts for five consecutive days. This work rate represented 110 percent of his power output and 108 percent of his heart rate (166 beats per minute) at maximal steady state. As you can see, the rider was able to maintain or nearly maintain the required power output for the first four of the five training days. However, the heart rate dropped progressively from the first through the fourth day, even though the work rate was maintained. In fact, by the fourth day, the rider's heart rate was only 101 percent of his maximal steady state heart rate. By relying solely on heart rate data, athletes in this situation could reach two possible conclusions, both of them wrong. First, they might conclude that they are incapable of performing consecutive days of intervals; or second, they might try to push harder on the second or third day of intervals in order to attain the "proper" heart rate. This strategy would almost certainly result in an intensity that would cause an athlete to "blow up" before the workout could be completed.

One very important aspect of training is knowing just how hard to push before backing off and taking time to recover. If you push too much, you may become stale and run the risk of overtraining. Push too little, and you will never reach your potential. Devices that monitor power output take some of the guesswork out of this process and make coaching a little less of an art and a little more of a science. The previous case offers a prime example of this point, as the rider was clearly capable of performing the prescribed work for four consecutive days, but by the fifth day he had ex-

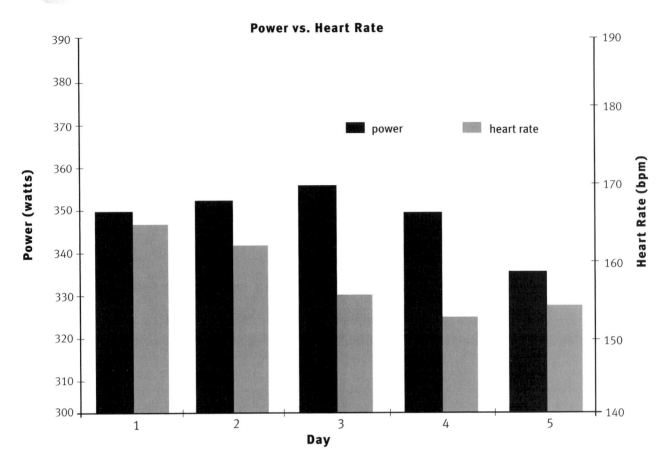

Power outputs and heart rates for three-minute intervals performed on five consecutive days. Although the rider could maintain the proper power output for four of the five days, the prescribed heart rate was maintained only for the first day. Performing supermaximum sustainable power intervals (see page 62) on a trainer can help maintain proper workloads.

ceeded his limit and would have been better served by using that day for recovery.

Regardless of the method you use to monitor your work intensity, take the time to learn how to use the instrument properly. It is not enough to know how to turn on the monitor and collect data. To get the most out of these training tools you also must understand what the data are telling you about your body. If you need assistance, seek the advice of an exercise physiologist or a qualified coach who can help you get the most out of your workouts.

CHAPTER 6

Choosing Workouts

Core Workouts

This chapter presents the eight core workouts you will use to formulate the majority of your training program. Each workout is described in terms of duration and intensity. With the exception of the sprint and leadout intervals, the intensities are based on your MSS and MSPO data. The information from your MSS test is used to prescribe your workout intensities based on the five training zones shown below.

TRAINING ZONE INTENSITIES

TRAINING ZONE	PERCENT OF MSS HEART RATE OR MSPO
1	65–75
2	76–85
3	86–95
4	96–105
5	ABOVE 105

The chapter concludes with an overview of the relatively new technique of block training.

Recovery Ride

Duration: 30 to 60 min.
Intensity: Zones 1 to 2 (65 to 85 percent of MSS heart rate or MSPO)
Purpose: To speed recovery from previous workouts. Brief, low-intensity rides can improve recovery rates by increasing the blood flow to working muscles without placing those muscles under excessive stress. Increasing blood flow to the working muscle also increases the delivery of both carbohydrates to help restore muscle glycogen and proteins for use in repairing muscle tissue.

Long, Slow Distance

Duration: 2 to 8 hr.
Intensity: Zones 2 to 3 (76 to 95 percent of MSS heart rate or MSPO)
Purpose: To strengthen the cardiovascular system, improve the aerobic capacity of the recruited muscles, and increase the muscle stores of glycogen and fat. Long endurance rides primarily tax the slower-twitch muscle

fibers, although faster-twitch fibers can be recruited as slower-twitch fibers become fatigued. These workouts strengthen the heart and increase blood volume and red blood cell mass, adaptations that enhance oxygen and nutrient delivery to the working muscle and promote more efficient removal of waste products such as carbon dioxide and hydrogen ions. Finally, long endurance rides increase the amount of aerobic enzymes and the number of mitochrondria in the stimulated fibers.

Maximum Sustainable Power (MSP) Intervals

Duration: 8 to 30 min.
Intensity: High zone 4 (100 to 105 percent of MSS heart rate or MSPO)
Work to Rest Ratio: about 2:1
Purpose: To increase work tolerance at and slightly above MSPO. Physiologically, these workouts promote many of the same effects as long endurance rides, only to a much greater degree. In addition, pathways that produce and consume lactic acid are utilized more extensively. Faster-twitch fibers are more involved during MSP intervals and become more aerobically trained. The greater overall training stimuli induces a larger training effect, resulting in a better-conditioned athlete. These intervals can be done on the road or a stationary trainer. Cadences should be similar to those encountered in competitive situations. Also, it is wise to do these intervals on both flat terrain and long, gradual climbs where available.

Supermaximum Sustainable Power (SMSP) Intervals

Duration: 1 to 6 min.
Intensity: Zone 5 (more than 105 percent of MSS heart rate or MSPO)

Work to Rest Ratio: Typically 1:1, but will vary depending on objectives
Purpose: To increase MSPO and work capacity at nonsustainable work rates. The intensity of these intervals improves both the aerobic and anaerobic capacities of practically all muscle fiber types. Like MSP intervals, SMSP intervals increase capillary density, blood volume, and red blood cell mass. They also improve lactate and hydrogen ion management and increase numbers of mitochondria. These training effects help an athlete maintain higher power outputs for longer periods of time and improve his or her performance in activities such as time trialing and making or chasing down breaks. These intervals are very difficult to endure, but are probably the most important workouts in the competitive cyclist's training program. Cadences should be similar to those encountered during road racing and time trialing events. Because of the high intensity, SMSP intervals are best done on a trainer where there a fewer opportunities to "cheat."

Muscle Endurance Intervals

Duration: 8 to 20 min.
Intensity: Zone 3 to low zone 4 (86 to 99 percent of MSS heart rate or MSPO)
Work to Rest Ratio: 1–2:1
Purpose: To increase the aerobic endurance capacity of faster-twitch fibers and to increase power at low cadence. Muscle endurance intervals are best performed on a stationary trainer or a long hill. Choose a gear that will allow you to achieve the required intensity while maintaining a cadence of approximately 50 rpm. The low cadence will require a very forceful contraction, resulting in the recruitment of faster-twitch muscle fibers. The duration of the intervals combined with the relatively high volume of work will result in faster-twitch fibers with greater endurance capacity.

Leadout Intervals

Duration: 10 to 30 sec.
Intensity: Identical to a fast leadout in a race; just below a sprinting intensity
Work to Rest Ratio: 1:1
Purpose: To increase the endurance capacity of the faster-twitch muscle fibers. The high intensity and high cadence of these intervals, combined with incomplete recovery periods, stimulate faster-twitch fibers to become more aerobic without compromising their explosiveness. The result is a powerful fiber that also possesses great endurance.

Leadout intervals are best performed on a stationary trainer. Begin each effort from a rolling start at a cadence of 60 rpm. At the start of each interval, accelerate your cadence as quickly as possible to 120 to 130 rpm and maintain this cadence for the duration of the work interval. Choose a gear that is large enough to be somewhat difficult to accelerate, but not so large that you are unable to reach and maintain at least 120 rpm for at least the last half of the interval. Remain seated for the duration of the work intervals.

Sprint Intervals

Duration: 10 to 15 sec.
Intensity: Full sprint
Work to Rest Ratio: 1:6–9
Purpose: To develop explosive power and sprinting ability. These intervals are best performed on a stationary trainer or on a slight uphill grade. Begin each interval from a dead stop (or slow roll if on the road) and accelerate as quickly as possible to terminal velocity. Choose a gear that provides a difficult start but is not so large that you cannot reach a cadence of 130 to 140 rpm by the end of the work interval. As with the leadout intervals, remain seated for the duration of the sprint intervals.

Group Rides

Duration: Unlimited
Intensity: Variable
Work to Rest Ratio: Not applicable
Purpose: Group rides provide an opportunity to participate in practice races and serve a number of purposes. By riding in a group, cyclists can practice their group riding skills such as drafting, echelons, pacelines, and bunch sprinting. Race strategies that require other riders, such as breaking away and chasing down breaks, can also be practiced when riding in a group of motivated riders. Moderately paced group rides can provide companionship on long endurance rides. Likewise, fast-paced competition can provide motivation for a rider who needs to do a lot of high-intensity work.

When choosing a group ride, be sure it will meet your immediate training needs. I frequently see cyclists go on group rides only to do the wrong type of workout for that particular day. It's easy to get sucked into what the group is doing, to do a hard workout when you really need an easy recovery ride or to do several hours at a moderate pace when short, high-intensity intervals are what you need. Therefore, be careful when choosing a group, or have the discipline to go your own way.

Block Training

This relatively new training approach involves training very hard for several days in a row and then resting for several days to allow the body to recover and supercompensate. Frequently, to increase the training stress on the body, the same types of workouts are performed on each day of the training blocks. The theory behind block training is that overloading a single system and then allowing adequate rest will cause the system to supercompensate more than with traditional training strategies.

I first began experimenting with block training in 1989 when I was running the strength and conditioning program at the U.S. Olympic Training Center in Lake Placid, New York. This position gave me my first opportunity to apply the theories I had studied in the exercise physiology program at the University of Missouri. Before starting at the USOTC, I talked to a few strength coaches and read books on strength and conditioning techniques in hopes of improving my practical knowledge in this area. I grew disturbed by the many discrepancies between how scientists elicit increases in muscular size, strength, and power in the laboratory and techniques advocated in many publications to achieve these same training responses. In fact, many practical approaches not only lacked any objective evidence to support them, but also utilized methods that contradicted scientific knowledge of how muscle responds to exercise training.

A second problem I had with many of the traditional approaches to strength training was the length of time it took to achieve results. Many programs required three to four months to complete, which was simply not a practical option for athletes like cyclists who have brief off-seasons and spend a great deal of their in-season time on the bike. It was clear that I had to develop a strength-training method that would be effective and could be completed in a short period of time.

Based on these requirements and the knowledge I had of the type of work required to develop muscle size, strength, and power, I formulated a training plan, similar to that presented in chapter 7, that broke away from traditional resistance training programs in that it advocated rigorous training of the same muscle groups on consecutive days before allowing several days of recovery. At that time, this type of training was considered taboo by many strength and conditioning gurus. Many people scoffed at this new approach, citing the need for recovery and the high possibility of injury when the muscle is worked on consecutive days. While I agreed that the body requires a stressful stimulus followed by a recovery period to achieve a maximal training effect, I pointed out that almost no research had been done on optimal combinations of stress and recovery. As for the potential for injury, I believed that this regimen would pose little risk, based on the fact that for years scientists had elicited muscle growth in laboratory animals (with few ill effects) by having them perform heavy resistance training every day for weeks or even months at a time.

I put this plan into action by performing a weekly program of two consecutive days of heavy lifting, followed by a day off, two more days of heavy lifting, and then two days off. After three weeks, I had found that although lifting on the second day of a two-day block was taxing, I could perform the work. More importantly, I was able to complete the three weeks of strenuous training without injury. I followed this growth period with a two-week strength period and a two-week power period. Remarkably, after two complete cycles (about thirteen weeks) of this program, my *one repetition maximum* (the maximum weight I could lift for a single repetition) on the squat exercise increased from 185 pounds to 375 pounds, which was nearly three times my body weight at the time!

Since first developing this program in 1989 I have prescribed it to several hundred athletes from a variety of sports. All have seen significant gains in strength and power, and to date none has experienced an injury from this training approach.

Despite my success with block training in the weight room, I was hesitant to apply these principles to on-the-bike training for cyclists. At that time there were no practical devices to monitor the power output of cyclists training on their own bicycles, and heart rate data suggested that cyclists could not sustain multiple days of high-intensity training on a bicycle. However, I would soon learn that not only could cyclists maintain power outputs on consecutive days of hard training, but they also could attain a dramatic training effect from doing so.

In 1994 David Martin, a doctoral student from the exercise physiology department at the University of Wyoming, came to the USOTC in Colorado Springs to do research for his dissertation on the relationship between exercise stress, hormone levels, and overtraining. Martin set out to overtrain a group of category 1 and 2 cyclists by having them perform a high volume of high-intensity interval training for three weeks. During the first week of training the subjects performed seven interval sessions over a period of four consecutive days. The second and third weeks consisted of eight interval sessions over five consecutive days. Each day's training consisted of one hour of intervals performed at a workload that would elicit 85 to 100 percent of maximal heart rate. Each subject had his hormone levels and exercise performance monitored before, during, and after the three-week training period. Following the training program, the subjects were given a weeklong taper period during which their exercise performance and hormone levels were monitored.

Martin made three interesting observations over the course of the study. First, he found that when sufficiently motivated, the subjects could maintain high intensities even after four and five consecutive days of training. Second, at no time during the three-week training period did the subjects exhibit hormonal responses that would suggest overtraining.

Finally, despite the extreme training load, the subjects showed a remarkable improvement in exercise performance.

The results of Dave Martin's study and my own experiences in training athletes have left me with the following thoughts on block training.

1. Cyclists can maintain high-intensity training for several consecutive days if they are sufficiently motivated.

2. Training load should be reduced as a training block progresses.

3. Prolonged blocks of high-intensity training can be extremely effective in providing training overload.

4. Prolonged training blocks should be separated by periods of very light activity or complete rest to allow the body to recover from the training stimuli.

5. Regular rest periods of two to three days in a row will not compromise fitness or hinder an athlete's progress.

6. Regular two- or three-day periods away from the bike not only provide the body with the opportunity to recover, but also increase athletes' enthusiasm for training.

7. The term *overtraining* is frequently misused to describe an athlete who is simply tired or lacks enthusiasm for training.

Points 4 through 7 are very important ingredients in any training program, yet cyclists and coaches often overlook them. Athletes who do not make use of regular periods of reduced training load may experience reductions in their ability to respond to training and in their enthusiasm for workouts and competition.

Danny Pate's ability to produce and maintain a high power output has allowed him to win several national championships and one world championship.

CHAPTER 7

Preseason Training: The Four-Phase Plan

This chapter teaches you how to integrate the workouts and the block training approach presented in chapter 6 into a preseason training plan that will prepare you for the rigors of bicycle racing. The four-phase plan is designed to be performed almost entirely during the off-season. In its entirety, the plan requires approximately twenty to twenty-two weeks to complete, and should be scheduled so that the last two weeks of the final phase overlap with the start of the racing season. Thus, a rider who wishes to be racing in early March should begin the program no later than mid-October. However, you should add an extra week to ten days to the program to account for unforeseen interruptions caused by illness, work, or school.

Younger or lower-category riders who don't have high MSPOs should do the four-phase program in its entirety. Professional and elite-level amateur riders who have already established high MSPOs may wish to adjust the program to conform with their brief off-seasons. Many may wish to reduce the weight training portion of the program or integrate races into the program at an earlier time. However, even riders at this level who want to increase their MSPOs may want to consider delaying the start of their race season so that they can complete all four phases.

The Four-Phase Approach

As I have stated, the single most accurate predictor of success among competitive road racers is power output at maximal steady state. Although it does take great endurance to survive a road race that lasts for several hours, this typically is not the deciding factor in the outcome of the competition. More often what decides who wins or who is left to vie for the grand prize is the ability to separate oneself (either alone or with a group) from the rest of the field. Mari Holden demonstrated this in the 1999 Women's National Road Race in Cincinnati, Ohio. Mari was riding for the Italian Acca Due Lorena team and was in a break with two women from team Timex. With their superior numbers, it appeared that the Timex women had a definite advantage over Mari. However, the course at Cincinnati was incredibly demanding and favored strong riders. With several miles left, Mari attacked on the final steep climb and was able to ride away from the other women simply because they could not match her power output. Furthermore, Mari's ability to sustain a high power output kept her out in front of her two adversaries on the several miles of flat road between the crest of the climb and the finish line. Amazingly, Mari was able to stay ahead despite the combined efforts of the Timex women to catch her, and won her first national road racing title. A few hours later, I watched Danny Pate use his ability to produce and sustain a high power output to ride away from a decimated men's field on the same climb. Like Mari, Danny maintained his advantage, and won his first Senior National Road Championship.

To train your muscular system to produce greater power, you should use a training program with four sequential phases:

- weight training to increase the size, strength, and power of muscle tissue
- aerobic endurance training combining long, easy rides with leadout and muscle endurance intervals to improve cardiovascular conditioning and general endurance and increase the aerobic capacity of the faster-twitching muscle fibers
- intervals at power outputs above MSPO to increase power output in both sustainable and nonsustainable efforts
- intervals at MSPO to increase power output at MSS and capacity for high-intensity work

Each training phase (except for weight training) should be approximately three weeks long, followed by a rest period of five to seven days. During these rest periods, you should drastically reduce your workout volumes while maintaining some high-intensity work. A typical recovery period is shown in the table below.

There are two reasons for the regular rest periods. First, while the periods of work provide the training stimuli, periods of rest and relaxation allow the process of supercompensation to be completed. Athletes who ignore regular rest periods are not likely to ever realize the full training effect of their efforts. Second, when athletes do not take regular breaks in their

TYPICAL RECOVERY PERIOD	
DAY	**WORKOUT SCHEDULE**
1	OFF
2	OFF
3	1 TO 1½ HR. IN ZONES 1 TO 2
4	FIVE 1 MIN. SMSP INTERVALS FOLLOWED BY 1½–2 HR. IN ZONE 2
5	OFF
6	1½–2 HR. IN ZONES 1 TO 2
7	BEGIN THE NEXT TRAINING BLOCK

schedules they run a greater risk of losing their enthusiasm for training. This usually results in a drop in performance that often leads an athlete to believe he is overtrained. Once this false belief manifests itself, it can be very difficult for the athlete to accept that he is actually physically well and fully capable of performing at his top level. In the meantime, much training and conditioning can be lost and physical performance will suffer.

With few exceptions, you should follow this four-step approach to training in its entirety (see summary table). While the high-intensity intervals of the final two phases are where MSPO is

FOUR-PHASE PLAN SUMMARY

PHASE	NUMBER OF WEEKS	PURPOSE	MAJOR COMPONENTS
1. RESISTANCE TRAINING	TWO TO FOUR (HYPERTROPHY PERIOD)	STIMULATE MUSCLE GROWTH	HIGH LIFTING VOLUME, MODERATELY HIGH RESISTANCE
	TWO (STRENGTH PERIOD)	BUILD MUSCULAR STRENGTH	REDUCED LIFTING VOLUME, INCREASED RESISTANCE
	TWO (POWER PERIOD)	TRAIN MUSCLE TO PRODUCE GREAT FORCE AT FAST SPEEDS	INCREASED LIFTING SPEED, REDUCED RESISTANCE; SPRINT INTERVAL WORKOUTS
2. AEROBIC ENDURANCE	APPROX. THREE	BUILD AEROBIC AND ENDURANCE CAPACITIES OF CARDIO-PULMONARY AND MUSCULAR SYSTEMS, MAINTAIN POWER BUILT DURING RESISTANCE TRAINING	LONG, LOW-INTENSITY RIDES; SPRINT, LEAD-OUT, AND MUSCLE ENDURANCE INTERVALS
3. SUPERMAXIMUM SUSTAINABLE POWER INTERVALS	APPROX. THREE	BUILD CYCLING-SPECIFIC POWER OUTPUT	SHORT, VERY HIGH INTENSITY INTERVALS
4. MAXIMUM SUSTAINABLE POWER INTERVALS	APPROX. THREE	INCREASE HIGH-INTENSITY WORK CAPACITY	LONGER, HIGH-INTENSITY INTERVALS

built, the initial two phases provide you with the necessary fitness to get the most out of the final two phases. Therefore, you should avoid taking shortcuts during the first two phases, as this will ultimately hurt your ability to respond to the hard intervals of phases 3 and 4.

Phase 1: Resistance Training

The ability of muscle to produce powerful contractions is extremely important in the sport of cycling. Properly designed weight training programs can build the muscular size, strength, and power to support the repetitive and powerful muscular contractions needed by competitive riders. To understand the importance of a weight program designed specifically for cycling, you should become familiar with a few key terms and concepts.

Force. This refers to the ability of a muscle to create tension in order to push or pull against an object. Force can be *dynamic*, that is, producing movement, such as when a cyclist pushes and pulls against the pedals, causing the crank to rotate; or *static*, without movement, as in the force produced by the upper body and applied to the handlebars to maintain position on the bicycle. The maximum amount of tension a muscle can produce is limited by the size and number of the muscle's contracting fibers and the magnitude of nervous system stimulation causing these fibers to contract.

Work. Work is simply a product of the distance over which a particular force is applied (work = force × distance). For example, a certain amount of force must be applied to ride over a flat course 1 kilometer in length. However, if that 1-kilometer course was uphill, more force would be needed to propel the bicycle at the same speed, thus increasing the required amount of work. Likewise, if the distance of the course was increased, so would

be the amount of work required to ride over the course.

Strength. Synonymous with force, strength is the ability of a muscle to produce tension, resulting in the development of force. Strength can be increased by overloading the muscle with high resistances of the type typically encountered in weight training. Note that strength gains are speed specific; that is, strength is gained at contractile speeds equal to or less than the speed at which the muscle is trained. In other words, if your lifts are executed at slow speeds in the gym, you will increase your muscular strength at these slow speeds but not at the faster speeds required for pedaling a bicycle.

Power. Power, the amount of work that can be completed in a given amount of time, is equivalent to work ÷ time or force × distance ÷ time. Viewed simply, it is the ability to exhibit strength at high speeds. In a sport like bicycle racing where finishing order is dependent on the amount of time required to perform a certain amount of work, power is the most important of all these concepts.

Anatomy and Physiology of a Muscular Contraction

Recall from chapter 1 that muscles are made up of motor units composed of muscle fibers and the nerve that provides the contractile stimuli for those fibers. These motor units vary in size and composition (slower- or faster-twitching muscle fibers) based on the muscle's tasks. When the nervous system sends a signal through the nerve, the fibers of the motor unit create tension. When enough motor units are stimulated to create the necessary tension, the muscle shortens and movement occurs. The amount of force and power that can be produced by a particular muscle depends on the size and type of the fiber, the amount of tension the fiber is able to produce without being severely damaged, and the magnitude of the nervous impulse provided to the motor unit. Fortunately, all of these characteristics respond to training.

Designing an Effective Resistance Training Program

Upon hearing the term *resistance training* most cyclists think of going to the gym and lifting weights. While lifting weights is an important aspect of a resistance training plan, the program should include workouts on the bicycle as well as in the gym. The principle of *specificity of training* dictates that the most effective training closely resembles the requirements of competition. However, building muscles capable of producing the fast and powerful contractions needed by competitive cyclists requires muscle fibers strong enough to produce force quickly without being injured. An intense weight training program builds muscle fibers with these qualities most effectively. Once these foundations are laid, more-specific qualities can be gained through a combination of high-speed lifting in the weight room and on-the-bike workouts.

Muscular Adaptation to Resistance Training

Because strength gains are speed specific, a resistance training program should include periods of high-speed lifting to allow strength gains to transfer into increased power output on the bicycle. Given this fact, it may seem useless to weight train at anything other than fast speeds. However, high-speed weight training requires the generation of large forces and places the muscles under great stress. To withstand this stress without injury, the muscle must be well conditioned. Therefore, a resistance training program should include phases designed to develop muscle size, strength, and power.

Development of Muscular Size

Muscular strength is highly correlated with muscle size. Larger muscle fibers, like larger tubes on a bicycle frame, are stronger and less susceptible to damage. Most strength and conditioning coaches agree that muscle tissue will grow larger after being subjected to overload followed by periods of rest and recovery. Traditional approaches to weight training reflect these beliefs by instructing athletes to follow each day in the weight room with a day of rest. While this one day on, one day off approach is widely accepted by the strength and conditioning community, there is little scientific evidence to suggest that it is the best strategy for increasing muscle size.

In contrast to the traditional approach, experimental techniques used by researchers to elicit muscle growth are typically far more rigorous. These models impose a higher number of muscle contractions against relatively high resistances, and clash with traditional strategies by requiring the subjects to perform several consecutive days of lifting without any days off to allow the muscles to recover. Despite their departure from conventional techniques, these experimental models elicit significant increases in muscle size in relatively short periods of time, frequently in as little as two weeks, and in general, they appear to be far superior in stimulating muscle growth than traditional approaches.

Based on this information, a sensible program for increasing muscle size would require extreme overload through moderately high resistances and many muscle contractions and should last at least two weeks. And though there is disagreement regarding the necessity of rest periods, it's probably wise to include some days of rest to avoid staleness.

Increasing Muscular Strength

The second aspect of a successful resistance training program involves increasing the strength and resilience of the muscle fibers and the intensity of the nervous impulses that reach them. By increasing the size of the muscle fibers in the initial period of the program you will increase their strength, thereby increasing their ability to produce force and making them less susceptible to injury. In addition, improving the nervous system's ability to transmit more-intense impulses allows the muscle to create more-forceful contractions. Thus, training the nervous system is as important to increasing muscular strength as is training the muscle.

The nervous system's involvement in a muscle contraction has two components, stimulation and inhibition. *Nervous system stimulation* involves the amount of stimulation provided to a motor unit's muscle fibers, which signals them to contract. Increasing the number and/or magnitude of impulses sent to the motor units can increase the force developed by a contracting muscle. *Nervous system inhibition* inhibits or reduces nervous system stimulation. This functions as a safety mechanism to reduce the possibility of muscle injury. The inhibitory system is composed of tension receptors within each muscle. Once a muscle develops a certain amount of tension, the receptors are stimulated and provide negative feedback to the nervous system, reducing the impulses sent to the muscle and decreasing the force of contraction. Because of nervous system inhibition, a muscle's true maximal force is rarely produced. However, people have exhibited superhuman strength in unusually stressful situations, presumably by subconsciously overriding nervous system inhibition. A person's ability to lift a car to free a trapped loved one is a dramatic example of the potential of the human muscular system.

Fortunately, the nervous system stimulation and inhibition systems can be altered with training. Providing adequate overload to the muscle can increase nervous system stimulation and the stimulation threshold of the tension receptors, which will increase the amount of force the muscle can produce before the process of nervous system inhibition is activated.

Proper training to increase muscular strength and nervous system efficiency involves maximally stimulating the system with very high resistance. The number of sets and number of repetitions per set are reduced relative to the growth phase and the resistances are increased to near maximum. Quality of work is stressed over quantity during the strength phase, as the muscle is required to do less total work and is given more recovery time between sets and workouts.

Increasing Muscular Power

While training with relatively high resistance is an effective way of increasing muscle size and strength, contraction speeds during high-resistance training are generally much slower than those experienced during competition. Because strength gains are specific to the speeds at which the muscle is trained, little of the strength gained during the first two phases will carry over to increased performance on the bicycle. Therefore, during the power phase you will utilize relatively low-resistance, high-speed lifts to transfer the strength you gained during the growth and strength phases to strength at speeds that will increase your cycling performance. As in the strength phase, the total work volume is low and recovery time is increased to improve the quality of each lift. During the power phase you should also begin sprint intervals at least once a week as a more specific activity to develop power.

Maintenance of Strength and Power Gains

Once you complete the strength program, you'll need to perform few if any structured weight room workouts. While it is true that you will lose strength if you do not continue with weight workouts throughout the year, your ultimate goal should be getting faster on the bike and not necessarily stronger in the weight room. Weight workouts will serve you well in building muscular strength and power, but there comes a point in each year when you are better served by focusing on other aspects of training. Also keep in mind that your muscles don't know the difference between pushing against a barbell and pushing against a bicycle pedal, and your upcoming training will contain a great deal of muscle endurance, sprint, and leadout intervals. These workouts can be thought of as on-the-bike resistance training, as they require a great deal of strength and power.

Sample Program

The following resistance program is divided into four phases that together make up a cycle. The program requires three weeks of preparation lifting, two to five weeks dedicated to building muscular size, two weeks for increasing muscular strength, and a final two weeks to develop muscular power. Resistances for each cycle are based on your one repetition maximum (1 RM), the greatest amount of weight you can lift for one repetition for each prescribed lift. Begin the cycle with a preparation phase in which you lift three times per week for three weeks. During the first week, do two sets of eight reps per set with very light weights for each exercise. The importance of using light weights for the first three sessions cannot be overstressed, as using weights that are too heavy will encourage poor form and result in extreme muscle soreness that may inhibit your ability to lift on subsequent days. Increase your workload during the second week by upping the number of sets to three and gradually increasing the weight. During the third week, continue to increase the amount of weight and raise the number of sets to four per exercise.

Setting Your One Repetition Maximum

Once you have completed the preparation phase, the next step is setting a one repetition maximum for each of your lifts. But before you rush off to the gym, consider the order in which you'll be performing your lifts since this will affect your results. Because setting a 1 RM is difficult, you may wish to spread out your lifts over several days to avoid fatigue and assure the most accurate results. When you're in the gym, the first lift should be the one that works the largest muscles, the most muscle groups, and requires the most complex movements. Since the back squat utilizes more large muscle groups (the legs, gluteals, and lower back) than any other lift and also is the most complex lift you'll perform, you should do this lift first.

Another consideration is to avoid targeting the same muscle groups on consecutive exercises. Targeting different muscle groups minimizes muscle fatigue, ensuring more accurate assessments of muscle strength. Thus, after performing the back squat, your next lift should target the muscles of the upper body. Two examples are the latissimus pull-down or the inclined dumbbell press. Following this upper-body lift, you would then return to a lower-body exercise, like the hamstring curl or the leg press.

After you have devised a suitable lifting schedule, begin your one repetition maximum session with the warm-up and stretching routine presented later in this chapter. The 1 RM attempts for each lift should be preceded by a warm-up set for that particular lift. Six to eight repetitions at a similar weight to that used during the final week of the preparatory period should be sufficient. Once the warm-up set has been completed, increase the resistance and attempt one repetition against this new weight. Since it is undesirable to fail on your first attempt, use a weight that is challenging but well within your ability. If you successfully complete a single repetition, increase the weight and allow yourself two to three minutes of rest before you attempt the new resistance. Continue this strategy until you are unable to perform one repetition against a new resistance (ideally, this should occur within four to five attempts). At this point, record the weight from your heaviest successful attempt and move on to the next lift.

Above all, be safety conscious when in the weight room and take time during the preparatory phase to learn proper lifting technique. Setting a 1 RM can be extremely rigorous and thus increases the danger for all lifters. Thus, utilize the necessary safety procedures to decrease the likelihood of injury. Because one rep max tests require you to fail, have a friend spot you when lifting free weights and wear a weight belt during the back squat to protect your lower back. Finally, rigorous weight lifting is not recommended for everyone. Individuals suffering from hypertension, degenerative joint disease, or who have previous joint or muscle injuries may want to reconsider before deciding to embark on an intense weight training program.

Period 1: Hypertrophy

The purpose of the hypertrophy period is to stimulate muscle growth by requiring a high number of repetitions against moderately high resistances. Due to the high work volume, during this period lifting should take priority over riding. In fact, it is preferable to stop riding or at least decrease your volume on the bike during the hypertrophy period. Furthermore, the extreme load provided by the hypertrophy period will push many riders to their limit, so you should pay close attention to your response. While a certain amount of soreness and discomfort is expected, if you develop chronic soreness, especially in the joints, decrease the training load by reducing the resistance or number of sets performed.

Hypertrophy period workout specifications
Duration: 2 to 4 weeks
Frequency, lower body: 4 days per week (2 heavy days, 2 light days); on light days, reduce resistances by five percentage points (e.g., 65 percent of 1 RM becomes 60 percent). Each week lower-body lifts are performed two days on, one day off, two days on, two days off (e.g., Monday and Thursday, on; Wednesday, off;

HYPERTROPHY PERIOD

SETS	REPS	PERCENT OF 1 RM	REST BETWEEN SETS (MIN.)
#1 AND #2	10 TO 12	65	1½ TO 2
#3 AND #4	10 TO 12	70	1½ TO 2
#5 AND #6	10 TO 12	75	1½ TO 2

Thursday and Friday, on; Saturday and Sunday, off). Heavy days (Mondays and Thursdays) should follow rest days and light days (Tuesdays and Fridays) should follow heavy days.

Frequency, upper body: 2 days per week (1 heavy day, 1 light day); on light days, reduce resistances by five percentage points (e.g., 65 percent of 1 RM becomes 60 percent). Each week upper-body lifts are performed on Mondays and Thursdays or Tuesdays and Fridays. Reduce the number of sets to three. Because it's unnecessary and even undesirable to build large amounts of muscle mass in the upper body, restrict each upper body lift to one set for each resistance (e.g., one set at 65 percent of 1 RM, one set at 70 percent, etc.), for a total of three sets for each lift.

Period 2: Strength

The purpose of the strength period is to over-load the muscle with high resistances to recruit the maximal number of motor units and require high levels of nervous system involve-ment. During the strength period, lifting volume is reduced and resistance is increased.

Strength period workout specifications

Duration: 2 weeks
Frequency: 2 days per week (1 heavy day, 1 light day)

STRENGTH PERIOD WEEK 1			
SETS	REPS	PERCENT OF 1 RM	REST BETWEEN SETS (MIN.)
#1	6	70	2
#2	6	75	2
#3	6	80	2
#4	6	85	2

STRENGTH PERIOD WEEK 2			
SETS	REPS	PERCENT OF 1 RM	REST BETWEEN SETS (MIN.)
#1	5	85	2
#2	4	90	2
#3	3	95	2
#4	2	100	2

Period 3: Power

The purpose of the power period is to train the muscle to produce great force at fast speeds. Resistances are reduced and lifting speed is increased to mimic contractile speeds experienced while riding. During this period you should also begin to perform sprint interval workouts (see page 63), which will provide a highly specific workout to further develop your muscular power.

Note: Generally, the fast contractions experienced during competition are limited to the lower extremities, so it is not necessary to perform upper body lifts during the power period. Instead, continue the upper-body lifts with a second strength period.

Power period workout specifications
Duration: 2 weeks
Frequency: 3 days per week (1 heavy day,

POWER PERIOD SAMPLE WEEKLY SCHEDULE

DAY	WORKOUT SCHEDULE
MONDAY	HEAVY
TUESDAY	1 HR. EASY RIDE
WEDNESDAY	SPRINT INTERVALS
THURSDAY	EASY/OFF
FRIDAY	LIGHT
SATURDAY	2 HR. EASY RIDE
SUNDAY	1½ HR. EASY RIDE

POWER PERIOD WEEKS 1 AND 2

SETS	REPS	PERCENT OF 1 RM	REST BETWEEN SETS (MIN.)
#1	8	45	2
#2	6	50	2
#3	4	55	2
#4	3	60	2

1 light day); work each muscle group each day with at least one day of active rest between workouts (e.g., Monday and Friday, weights; Wednesday, sprint intervals).

Performing Your Resistance Training Workout

Each weight workout should begin with an extensive warm-up and stretching routine. Lifting heavy weights places muscles under a great deal of strain and can result in injury. Flexible muscles are less prone to injury, and good overall flexibility can improve your posture both on and off the bike. Warm up by doing some form of light aerobic activity before beginning your stretching routine. Warming the muscle improves its flexibility and increases the effectiveness of stretching.

Perform the stretches slowly and only to the point of mild discomfort. Once you reach this point, hold the stretch for twelve to fifteen seconds. Avoid fast movements or bouncing, as these actions can evoke a *stretch response*, a protective mechanism in which muscle fibers contract in an attempt to prevent a strained or torn muscle. (See pages 78–81 for photographs and captions of all stretches.)

After completing the stretching routine, proceed to the lifting portion of the workout. The resistance training workout requires only six basic lifts. While it is somewhat rudimentary compared to the lifting programs of many other sports, the essential movements in cycling are relatively simple and do not require a wide variety of lifts. Also note that some of the lifts will not be performed in all three lifting periods.

Begin each workout with the most complex lift (the back squat, shown on page 82) and progress toward the simpler lifts such as the hamstring curl. Complex lifts require coordination and balance and typically recruit more muscle groups than simple, single-joint lifts. By doing the complex lifts when you are relatively fresh, you'll be better able to maintain proper lifting form and perform the lifts effectively. Thus, the lifts should be completed in the order presented. Finally, do not skip any of the lifts, as this may create strength imbalances that could lead to injury.

Begin each weight workout with a warm-up. Ten minutes of light aerobic exercise will increase the flexibility of your muscles and prepare them for the rigors of a weight workout.

Shoulder stretch. *Grasp your upper arm just above the elbow. Pull the elbow toward the back of your head. Then switch sides.*

Upper back stretch. *Grasp your arm at the elbow and pull the arm horizontally to your chest. Then switch sides.*

Chest stretch. *Place the palm of your hand flat against the wall at the height of your shoulder. Rotate your chest away from the wall until you feel a stretch in your upper chest. Then switch sides.*

Inner thigh stretch. *Kneel on both knees. Extend one leg to the side and bend your body sideways toward the outstretched leg until you feel a stretch in the upper portion of the inner thigh of your outstretched leg. Then switch sides.*

Front hip stretch. *Kneel with one knee on the ground. Extend your opposite leg and place your foot flat on the floor (left). While keeping your torso straight, move your upper body forward and down. You* should feel a stretch in the front of the hip and upper thigh. Then switch sides. Avoid leaning your torso forward (right).

Hamstring stretch. *Sit with both legs extended in front of your body. Maintain erect posture in your upper body by keeping your shoulders back and your back straight. Begin the stretch by leaning forward* at the hips *while keeping your knees straight. To do the stretch properly, visualize yourself pushing* your chest toward your knees while maintaining a straight back (left). Do not reach out with your hands to grab your toes (right); this causes you to bend at the waist, which does nothing to increase the stretch on the hamstring and places unnecessary strain on the lower back.

Medial hip rotator. *Sit with the soles of your feet together. Press your legs down toward the floor until you feel a stretch in the groin.*

Lateral hip rotator. *Sit with your legs in front of you, your knees bent at approximately 90 degrees, and your feet flat on the floor, slightly wider than your shoulders. Force one knee inward and down by rotating your thigh at the hip. You should feel the stretch on the outside of your hip. Then switch sides.*

Upper hamstring and gluteal stretch. *Lie on your back and grasp your lower thigh just above the knee. Pull your thigh toward your shoulder. Then switch sides. Avoid grasping the front of the upper shin; this places the knee at an acute angle and may damage the knee joint.*

Abdominal and anterior spine stretch. *Lie on your stomach and use your arms to press your upper body off the floor. Because cyclists spend a great deal of time bending forward at the waist, they are vulnerable to tightness in the muscle and connective tissues along the anterior portion of the spine. This stretch is especially effective in stretching these tissues.*

Quadriceps stretch. Grasp the front of your ankle and pull your foot up and away from your body. Then switch sides. Avoid pulling the foot toward the back as this places the knee at an acute angle and may damage the knee joint. This stretch can be performed standing (left) or lying down (right).

Lower leg stretch. Place the palms of your hands flat against the wall. Bend the knee of one leg. Slide the other leg back until you feel a stretch in your calf (left). Maintain this posture for twelve to fifteen seconds and then bend the knee of the outstretched leg, which moves the stretch down the leg toward the Achilles tendon (right). Maintain this new posture for twelve to fifteen seconds. Then switch sides.

Back squat. This exercise is probably the most cycling specific of all the lifting exercises and should be an integral part of any lifting program for cyclists. The back squat should be performed during each of the three lifting phases (hypertrophy, strength, and power).

Note: Due to the involvement of the lower back in the exercise, you should wear a weight belt whenever lifting at or above 80 percent of your 1 RM.

During the power phase, lifting form for the back squat is slightly modified. Complete the upward phase of the lift as quickly as possible and jump off the floor as high as you can. Because of the high lifting speeds during the power period, protect your shoulders with a towel or a bar pad when doing this exercise.

Stiff-legged dead lift. This lift strengthens the gluteal and hamstring muscle groups. It also increases the static strength of the lower back and can be effective in reducing lower back fatigue and soreness during long rides. In addition, the stiff-legged dead lift increases

Back squat. The back squat begins with proper posture. Place your feet shoulder-width apart. Keep your shoulders back, your chest out, and your head in a neutral position for the duration of the lift. Position the bar on your shoulders so that if it fell through your body it would land on your instep. Maintain this bar position throughout the lift.

The lift is initiated by flexion at the hips followed quickly by knee flexion. These actions force the pelvis back in a motion similar to that of sitting in a chair.

Continue until the backs of your thighs are parallel to the floor, maintaining proper upper body posture throughout the lift. Then return to the starting position.

hamstring and gluteal flexibility, which can help you attain more-aerodynamic positions for time trialing.

You should not use the traditional one repetition maximum strategy with the stiff-legged dead lift, nor should you follow the high-volume schedule of the hypertrophy period. Muscular fatigue and the use of heavy weights encourage poor form and increase the likelihood of lower back injuries.

Stiff-legged dead lift. When performing this lift, position your hands approximately shoulder-width apart, with your feet just inside a vertical plane running through each hand.

Keep your chest out and your shoulders back. There should be a slightly exaggerated inward curve in your lower back. Keep your knees slightly flexed throughout the lift.

Initiate the lift by flexing at the hip joints. Maintain your upper body posture and keep your head up throughout the lift.

Continue the downward phase of the lift until you reach the limit of hamstring flexibility, then return to the upright position. Should you pass the limit of hamstring flexibility, the inward curve of your lower back will disappear, causing unnecessary and potentially dangerous lower back strain.

Perform the stiff-legged dead lift throughout the weight training phase, limiting yourself to three or four sets of eight repetitions. Resistances should be challenging, but not so heavy that you cannot maintain proper form. As your ability to perform the lift improves, gradually increase the resistance, but avoid the extreme resistances of the strength period.

Finally, there is no power period for the stiff-legged dead lift, as high-speed lifting should be avoided.

Inclined dumbbell press. This upper body lift develops the muscles of the arms, shoulders, and upper chest. These muscles play an important role in sprinting, climbing, and maintaining proper posture while riding.

Inclined dumbbell press. Perform this on a bench with a horizontal angle of 45 to 60 degrees. Begin the lift with the bars of the dumbbells approximately level with your nose and your hands slightly wider than shoulder-width apart (photos at left). Your feet should be flat on the floor and you should maintain a natural curve in your lower back. Press the dumbbells directly upward until they meet above your head (below). Return to the starting position.

Perform the inclined dumbbell press throughout the weight training phase. Because excessive upper body muscle mass is undesirable in cycling, during the hypertrophy period you should only do one set of each of the prescribed resistances (three sets for each exercise) for upper body lifts. Also, because cycling does not require high-speed contractions from the muscles of the upper body, you don't need to implement a high-speed power period for these exercises. Instead, continue doing the upper body lifts during the power period by repeating the strength period of the lifting program.

Inclined leg press. Perform this lift during the hypertrophy and strength phases. The inclined leg press is designed to increase the size and strength of the quadriceps, gluteal, and hamstring muscle groups. Because you do not have to balance the weight and your lower back is not stressed, you can lift more weight on the leg press than with the back squat, which allows you to gain more strength in the muscles of the lower extremities.

Inclined leg press. Place your feet shoulder-width apart with your toes pointed straight ahead. Begin by lifting the weight off the pegs. Keep your legs nearly straight and avoid locking your knees.

Lower the weight until the knee joint reaches approximately 90 degrees. Return to the starting position.

Latissimus pull-down, rear view. Place your hands in a wide position, utilizing an overhand grip.

Latissimus pull-down, front view. Pull downward until the bar is level with the collarbone. Return to the starting position.

Latissimus pull-down. This exercise develops the muscles of the upper back to assist in sprinting, climbing, and the maintenance of posture. Perform the latissimus pull-down throughout the weight training period, substituting a second strength period for the power period.

Hamstring curl. This develops the hamstrings. Cycling builds very strong quadri-ceps, but when strong quadriceps are paired with weak hamstrings, knee and hamstring injuries are more likely to occur. Strengthening the hamstrings helps maintain a proper strength balance between these two muscle groups and reduces the chance of injury. Perform this lift throughout the weight training period.

Hamstring curl. To position yourself properly, begin by aligning the axis of rotation of your knee joints with the axis of rotation of the resistance arm of the machine.

Next, adjust the pad of the resistance arm low on your legs, near your ankles.

Begin the lift with your legs extended. Flex your knees until the pad of the resistance arm touches the backs of your thighs. Return to the starting position.

Exercises to Strengthen the Midsection

The muscles of the abdomen and lower back are extremely important to any activity. Cyclists rely on a strong midsection to maintain posture and stabilize the body for each pedal stroke. Building a strong midsection requires time and effort, but the benefits are well worth the costs. The exercises presented below are designed to work the upper and lower abdominals, the oblique muscles on the side of the lower torso, and the muscles of the lower back. To develop adequate midsection strength, I rec-ommend doing at least sixty repetitions of each exercise. While it is best if you can do all of the repetitions for each exercise in one set, splitting the reps into two or three sets is fine. The important thing is for you to do them each time you're in the weight room and continue to do them at least three times per week throughout the year. If you have other exercises you prefer, make sure you are isolating each of the four areas with equal amounts of volume (e.g., for each repetition that targets the upper abdomen, a repetition should be done for the lower abdomen, the obliques, and the lower back).

Abdominal crunch. Raise your legs to protect your lower back (left). Do not place your legs flat on the floor or have someone hold your feet to the floor. Raise your shoulders off the floor (right) and then return to the starting position.

Leg raises. Raise your feet so your hip joint is at a 90-degree angle (left). To protect your lower back, place your hands just above your pelvis and lower your legs until you feel your lower back begin to arch (right), then stop and again raise your legs to the starting position.

Dynamic back extension. This exercise is designed to strengthen the muscles of the lower back. Proper positioning on the Roman chair is important. Adjust the length of the foot support so that your pelvis is fully supported by the forward support pad. Your iliac crests (the sharp bones on either side of the lower abdomen) should rest on the forward support pad. This position stabilizes the pelvis, reduces involvement of the gluteals and hamstrings, and forces the muscles of the lower back to execute the lift. Begin by flexing at the waist and moving your torso as far down as possible (top). Then extend at the waist until your torso is in a neutral position (left). Avoid overextending your torso. Weights can be used to increase the resistance for the back extension (right).

Static back extension. *If you don't have access to a Roman chair, the static back extension can be an adequate substitute. Lie face down and arch your back until your head, chest, lower legs, and feet are above the mat. Hold this position for fifteen to twenty seconds.*

Side extension. *Positioning for this is similar to the dynamic back extension in that the pelvis is stabilized and movement occurs at the waist.*

Begin by lowering your torso to the lowest possible point (left), then raise your upper body to a neutral position (right).

A Proper Transition to On-the-Bike Training

With the completion of the weight training program, you now have muscle fibers capable of producing powerful contractions. You now must shift your attention to improving your muscles' endurance capacity without losing the power gained during the resistance training phase. Building muscular endurance requires a number of physiological adaptations. A strengthened heart and increases in blood volume and capillary numbers are needed to deliver nutrients to the working muscle. Inside the muscle fibers themselves, myoglobin must be synthesized to assist in the transfer of oxygen from the blood into the muscle. Synthesis of ATP requires increases in numbers of mitochondria and the enzymes that catalyze the reactions of the energy pathway.

To achieve these adaptations, your on-the-bike training should consist of long, low-intensity rides in combination with intervals of varying length and intensity. But selecting the proper mix of volume and intensity can be a complex task. Concentrate too much on low-intensity volume, and you'll lose the power you worked so hard to build during the weight training phase. Perform too many intervals before establishing a fitness base, and you won't get optimal results from your interval training. To avoid these problems, your on-the-bike training should be divided into three phases: an aerobic volume phase; a high-intensity, low-volume interval phase; and a moderate-volume, moderate-intensity interval phase. Each of the three phases is designed to maintain the training effects from the previous phase(s) and to provide the level of conditioning required to meet the demands of your subsequent training. Thus, you must be especially vigilant in completing each workout to the best of your ability, as each three-week period helps you prepare your body to meet the requirements of the following training period.

Phase 2: Aerobic Endurance

In the second of your four preparation phases you should focus on building the aerobic and endurance capacities of your cardiopulmonary and muscular systems by taking long, low-intensity rides. In the early part of the aerobic endurance phase rides are relatively short (as little as two to three hours, depending on your ability), but their duration should increase as the training period progresses. The eventual length of these endurance rides will depend on your competitive level and the length of your upcoming races. Professional and elite amateur road racers who will be competing in long, single-day events and multiday stage races should be doing rides of six hours or more by the end of the endurance period. Category 3 and 4 riders, whose races are somewhat shorter, should strive to do four- to five-hour endurance rides before the endurance block is finished. Professional women road racers should do volumes similar to their male counterparts. While women's races on the national and international level are typically shorter than men's, there are a number of women's events that justify the high training volumes. Races like the Hewlett-Packard Women's Challenge and La Grande Boucle Feminine (the women's version of the Tour de France) are long, grueling events, and women competing in these races are well served to maintain high training loads during the endurance period. At the local and regional level, women's races are typically about 60 to 75 percent as long as the men's events, and women who race strictly at these levels can meet their needs by doing less volume than men. This is not to say that women are incapable of doing the higher training volume, but rides of this length are not necessary to be competitive at these levels.

Although the vast majority of your rides during the endurance phase are long, low-intensity efforts, you need to begin structured intervals during this phase. High-volume, low-intensity training rides do a great deal to improve your cardiovascular conditioning and overall endurance, but they do not optimally tax your faster-twitch muscle fibers and thus do not prepare them for the upcoming supermaximum sustainable power intervals. Furthermore, if you stimulate your faster-twitch fibers with low-intensity contractions only, they will lose much of the powerful, fast-twitching abilities they gained during the weight training period.

To optimally tax your faster-twitching fibers, you must integrate a combination of sprint, leadout, and muscle endurance intervals into the aerobic endurance phase. This will increase the endurance capacity of these fibers while maintaining their ability to produce powerful contractions. This ultimately leads to an increased work capacity and leaves you better prepared for the supermaximum sustainable power interval phase.

Using the block training technique, you can get the most out of these intervals by performing sprint intervals before the long ride on the first day of a training block and doing leadout or muscle endurance intervals toward the end of a long ride on the final day of the block. This approach allows you to perform the workout requiring the highest power output (sprint intervals) while still fresh and ensures that your faster-twitch fibers will retain their powerful twitch characteristics. And by performing the leadout and muscle endurance intervals at the end of a multiday training block, you will magnify the aerobic demands placed on the faster-twitching fibers by forcing them to work when they are already somewhat fatigued.

The table below shows the basic format for

TYPICAL ENDURANCE PERIOD	
DAY	WORKOUT SCHEDULE
1	SPRINT INTERVALS, THEN 4 HR. IN ZONES 2 TO 3
2	2½ HR. IN ZONES 2 TO 3, THEN MUSCLE ENDURANCE INTERVALS
3	EASY/OFF
4	EASY/OFF
5	SPRINT INTERVALS, THEN 4½ HR. IN ZONES 2 TO 3
6	3½ HR. IN ZONES 2 TO 3
7	2½ HR. IN ZONES 2 TO 3, THEN LEADOUT INTERVALS
8	EASY/OFF
9	EASY/OFF
10	EASY/OFF

ten days of training during the endurance period.

Of course, the actual volume of the endurance rides and the intervals will depend on your ability and how far along you are in the endurance phase, but the basic structure of the program should follow the above approach.

Phase 3: Supermaximum Sustainable Power Intervals

Phase 3 is probably the most important of the four preparatory training phases, as it is where riders build the majority of their cycling-specific power output. It is also undoubtedly the most grueling of the four phases. The total volume of training drops considerably during this phase, but the volume of high-intensity work increases markedly. Many of my new clients scoff at the low volume of this training phase, especially after coming off the endurance work in the previous weeks. Their flippant attitudes are quickly replaced by respect for these intervals as they discover just how difficult it is to finish the workouts. "Do they have to be so hard?" clients sometimes ask. I respond by telling them that bike racing is difficult, and if they are unwilling to push themselves to complete these workouts, perhaps they are in the wrong sport.

As a general guideline, the intensity for SMSP intervals is 105 percent of MSPO or MSS heart rate and above. This, however, is only a rough guideline, since the duration of the intervals will somewhat dictate the work rate you can maintain. Therefore, it is best to simply do these intervals at the highest intensity you can maintain for the length of the interval and the volume of the workout. For instance, you would almost certainly be able to maintain a higher power output for one-minute intervals than for five-minute intervals. Thus, you will need to do a bit of experiment-

ing to determine exactly what intensities you can tolerate for any given duration.

The approach used during the SMSP training phase should reflect the needs of the rider. Interval length, recovery time between intervals, and total work volume will depend on your abilities and needs. When I begin working with riders, I usually want to focus on improving their short-term power output before gradually increasing the amount of time they can maintain their power. Therefore, I have these riders perform SMSP intervals of three minutes and shorter during their first three-week SMSP phase. Conversely, a rider who already has a great deal of power will concentrate more on longer intervals or perform shorter intervals with less recovery time.

The total volume of SMSP interval workouts will vary depending on the competitive level of the athlete, the types of races they will be entering, how long they have been performing these types of workouts, and where they are in the training phase. Professional and elite amateur riders compete in races that require higher volumes of high-intensity work than category 3 or 4 riders, so they should strive to do a higher volume of work. Likewise, riders who focus on road races require a greater total work volume than those who compete primarily in criteriums. The key is to identify the requirements of your primary events and manipulate your training volume to mirror these requirements. Using an instrument like the SRM, or hiring a coach who knows how to interpret data from power meters, can help you determine how much high-intensity work is required to be competitive.

Supermaximum sustainable power intervals should be performed in block fashion, with the duration of the intervals decreased as the block progresses. For instance, during a three-day block you may want to do four-minute intervals on the first day, two-minute intervals on the second, and one-minute intervals on the last. This approach offers you a break by decreasing the duration of the intervals as you become more fatigued. Usually, you can maintain the total workout volume for the entire block as long as you decrease the interval length. Decreasing the interval length also allows you to maintain or even increase your power output as the block progresses.

The table below shows a typical approach to SMSP intervals.

As the table shows, during the SMSP phase your time on the bike is drastically reduced and you have plenty of time off. The training is of such high intensity that you are wise to take advantage of the rest days to recover and supercompensate. Remember, improvement in work capacity requires hard work *and* periods of rest and recovery. Thus, you should follow each block of interval work with an equal number of days of complete rest or easy recovery rides.

Phase 4: Maximum Sustainable Power Intervals

Now that you've increased your ability to produce power efforts of intermediate duration, it's time to shift your focus toward longer intervals of slightly lower intensity. This strategy will continue to develop your MSPO and also increase your capacity for high-intensity work. Typically, MSP intervals will range from eight to twenty minutes in length. The duration of the intervals as well as the total work volume will increase as this phase of training progresses. Like the previous phases, the total volume of work will depend on your abilities and goals.

TYPICAL SMSP INTERVALS

DAY	WORKOUT SCHEDULE
1	5 X 4 MIN. INTERVALS
2	10 X 2 MIN. INTERVALS
3	OFF
4	1 HR. IN ZONE 2
5	6 X 4 MIN. INTERVALS
6	8 X 3 MIN. INTERVALS
7	10 X 1 MIN. INTERVALS, 2 SETS
8	EASY/OFF
9	EASY/OFF
10	1 HR. IN ZONE 2

After the first week to ten days of the MSP phase, you will have gained the conditioning necessary to compete in early-season races. In fact, you should incorporate racing into your schedule, as MSP intervals are not only physically challenging but mentally difficult to complete. Racing provides ample motivation to endure long, strenuous efforts and breaks the monotony of interval workouts. However, remember that the purpose of racing during this period is to gain training opportunities. Competitive results are secondary, and you should even be willing to sacrifice results to ensure a suitable workout.

The table below shows a typical MSP intervals training period.

Notice that, as in SMSP intervals, the duration of MSP intervals decreases as each block progresses. This can provide a psychological lift to the rider, making the workouts more bearable on the second or third day of a block. Another trick to maintain intensity is to do the intervals late in the block while climbing. By monitoring power outputs with the SRM, I have noticed that riders are more capable of maintaining high power outputs while climbing. This is likely due to the fact that if a cyclist coasts on a climb, he or she must expend extra energy to regain the proper intensity. This problem is less pronounced on a flat road and thus the temptation to cheat is more inviting.

A couple of common problems can arise from MSP training. Because you spend a great deal of time at one intensity, you may see a reduction in your ability to surge and change intensities. Many riders describe the feeling as being a "bit flat." You can minimize this problem by incorporating racing into your training

TYPICAL MSP INTERVALS	
DAY	WORKOUT SCHEDULE
1	THREE 10 MIN. MSP INTERVALS
2	LEADOUT INTERVALS, THEN FOUR 8 MIN. MSP INTERVALS
3	EASY/OFF
4	EASY/OFF
5	THREE 12 MIN. MSP INTERVALS
6	RACE OR THREE 10 MIN. MSP INTERVALS
7	FOUR 8 MIN. MSP INTERVALS (CLIMBING)
8	EASY/OFF
9	EASY/OFF
10	1 HR. IN ZONE 2

schedule, thereby providing workouts with varied intensities. If no races are available, add sprint, leadout, and short SMSP intervals to the program to keep yourself from becoming flat.

A second pitfall to avoid during the MSP phase is staleness. The volume of high-intensity work increases markedly during this phase, which can result in fatigue and a general lack of enthusiasm for training. To avoid this problem, take advantage of your rest and recovery days. If this is not enough to overcome the problem, be willing to make adjustments in your training schedule. For instance, instead of performing a single three-week training phase, consider doing two, two-week phases separated by a week of rest and recovery. The time away from structured training will likely rekindle your enthusiasm for riding.

Questions and Answers

Q. A lot of coaches advocate the use of low-resistance, high-repetition weight training to build muscular endurance. Is this a good idea?
A. Although there are still a lot of unanswered questions regarding weightlifting and cycling, I don't believe that low-resistance, high-repetition lifting is putting your time in the weight room to the best use. The weight room is probably the best place to build muscular strength and short-burst muscular power. And while high-power muscular endurance can be improved with low-resistance, high-repetition lifting, muscular endurance intervals are probably a better workout for achieving this training effect.

Q. What is the best training strategy when afflicted with a cold? I have seen some people train when they are sick, while others stop training until they are well.
A. It depends on the situation. I typically advise my clients to stop training if they are sick because training through a cold can prolong the illness or even lead to a more serious condition such as pneumonia. By resting, athletes can help their bodies to recover from illnesses, allowing them to return to normal training as soon as possible. Should the cold occur in close proximity to an important event, training should be continued, albeit at a much lower volume. This approach will have minimal impact on recovery and still help to maintain fitness.

Races provide excellent training opportunities during the competitive season.

CHAPTER 8

Training during the Competitive Season

Once you begin a competitive cycling season, you generally reduce your formal training because your races will usually provide you with plenty of hard workouts. Still, you need to arrange workouts and races to help you pursue your intermediate- and long-term goals. A second factor to consider when devising an in-season training program is your standing as a rider. For example, riders already competitive with their peers would follow a different program than novice riders who struggle to keep up with the pack even on their best days. Stronger riders have the luxury of knowing that they have real chances of winning races if they are well trained and prepared. This advanced development allows these riders to focus on preparing to peak for a certain race or group of races. In contrast, cyclists who are getting dropped consistently have no realistic chance of winning an event and will likely contribute little to the success of a team. Riders in this situation would be wise to forgo peaking for specific events and instead follow a training program that will increase their MSPOs, making them consistently stronger performers. Without making this initial commitment, these riders will likely see their development stagnate.

Becoming a Stronger Rider: Developing Power during the Competitive Season

As I've stated, the most pronounced difference between elite cyclists and their subelite counterparts is the ability to produce and sustain high power outputs. One of the biggest mistakes novice riders make is not taking time to develop their MSPO. By not focusing on their power output, many riders fall into the "dime a dozen" category of athletes who ride well from time to time when their form is good but lack the consistency to break into the elite category.

Developing a high MSPO is not easy; it can take several months or even years of concentrating on high-intensity training. To make the task even more difficult, a rider who is truly focused on improving her or his MSPO frequently must be willing to sacrifice short-term competitive results. While it can be difficult to convince many athletes and their coaches to give up near-term results for the sake of development, I have seen countless examples of cyclists with exceptional talent who never realize their potential because they are more concerned with how they will race next week than how they will race next year. Consequently, these riders tend to make only limited progress toward their long-term goals.

An in-season training program designed to increase MSPO utilizes races and high-intensity intervals to provide a high volume of high-intensity work. The races and workouts should be arranged in block fashion, with the rider taking several days off during each training period to recover from the training blocks. The length of each training period should vary from two to three weeks. I find that as the racing season progresses, riders often respond better to shorter training periods due to the cumulative fatigue of the season. The table below shows a typical three-week training period.

Notice that very difficult interval workouts are frequently prescribed on days immediately preceding competitions. Though this practice is

THREE-WEEK IN-SEASON TRAINING PROGRAM FOR A BEGINNING RIDER

	MONDAY	TUESDAY	WEDNES-DAY	THURSDAY	FRIDAY	SATURDAY	SUNDAY
WEEK 1	SMSP INTERVALS: 3 SETS, 3X 3 MIN. ON, 3 MIN. OFF, 10 MIN. BETW. SETS	SMSP INTERVALS: 3 SETS, 4X 2 MIN. ON, 2 MIN. OFF, 10 MIN. BETW. SETS	SMSP INTERVALS: 4 SETS, 6X 1 MIN. ON, 1 MIN. OFF, 8 MIN. BETW. SETS	EASY/OFF	EASY/OFF	RACE OR HARD GROUP RIDE	RACE OR HARD GROUP RIDE
WEEK 2	EASY/OFF	EASY/OFF	SMSP INTERVALS: 3 SETS, 3X 3 MIN. ON, 3 MIN. OFF, 10 MIN. BETW. SETS	EASY/OFF	SMSP INTERVALS: 3 SETS, 3X 3 MIN. ON, 3 MIN. OFF, 10 MIN. BETW. SETS	RACE OR HARD GROUP RIDE	RACE OR HARD GROUP RIDE
WEEK 3	EASY/OFF	EASY/OFF	1 HR. IN ZONE 2	SMSP INTERVALS: 3 SETS, 4X 2 MIN. ON, 2 MIN. OFF, 10 MIN. BETW. SETS	SMSP INTERVALS: 4 SETS, 6X 1 MIN. ON, 1 MIN. OFF, 8 MIN. BETW. SETS	RACE OR HARD GROUP RIDE	EASY/OFF

not conducive to optimal performance in these competitions, remember that the goal is to increase MSPO and not necessarily to win or place well in races. Furthermore, by riding in competitions on the second or third day of a training block, you are provided not only with opportunities to do a lot of very hard work, but also with encouragement at a time when you are likely to be fatigued and low on motivation. By comparison, imagine trying to do high-intensity intervals on your trainer after a two-day stage race.

As for the races themselves, you should strive to be as aggressive as possible. Just sitting in the pack and letting others do the work may be the smart strategy for winning races, but it will not provide you with the high volume of high-intensity work needed to develop a high sustainable power output. Instead, you should attack as frequently as possible and be willing to sacrifice competitive placement in favor of the required training load.

Let your capabilities dictate the volume of the interval workouts and the duration of the intervals within the workout. For instance, if you are in desperate need of power, you would initially focus on leadout and supermaximum sustainable power intervals. These intervals should be no more than two minutes in length to allow for high power outputs. Once you develop the ability to produce power over short time periods, move on to longer SMSP intervals, or keep the length of the efforts the same and decrease the recovery time between the intervals. This strategy will increase the amount of time that you can endure high-intensity work, which will eventually lead to a higher MSPO. This contrasts with the strategy needed if you are capable of producing a lot of power in short efforts, but lack the ability to endure large volumes of this intensity or to maintain high power outputs in long, steady efforts. Typically, this is the profile of a poor time trialist who lacks the ability to break away from a group and usually fades toward the end of a long race. If you fall into this category you should initially increase your volume of SMSP intervals, which will increase your capacity for work above your MSPO. Once this ability has been improved, you would focus on maximum sustainable power intervals that utilize shorter rest periods. Thus, an important issue to remember when designing the in-season portion (or any portion) of your training program is to customize it to your needs.

Specializing for Types of Events and Peaking for Races

Once riders develop the ability to ride competitively within their peer group, they can shift their attention toward more-specialized training for specific types of races and events. Cyclists preparing for a particular race or type of event have to be aware of the demands of their chosen discipline. Different types of races place different demands on the athlete and require different training strategies. To illustrate this point, the SRM graphs on the next page show the power output of a cyclist with an MSPO of 293 watts. Both graphs show races of approximately the same length, requiring the same amount of work, and having an average power output of approximately 295 watts. However, the graphs show that the way the work is performed in the time-trial graph (top) is markedly different than in the criterium graph (bottom).

During the criterium, the work is performed in a series of short, high-intensity periods separated by periods of very low intensity work. In the time trial, however, the power output is much more consistent over the course of the

Power (watts)

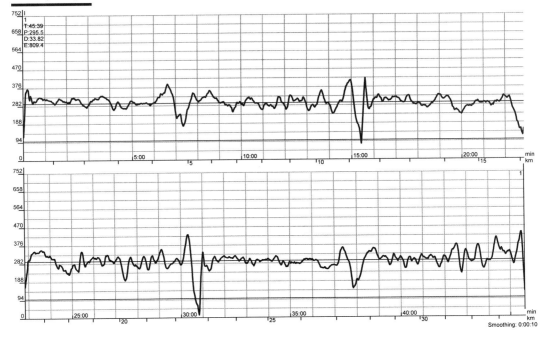

Although the total work and average power for this time trial (top) and criterium (bottom) are similar, the way the work is performed demonstrates the need for different training approaches for these two racing disciplines.

Power (watts)

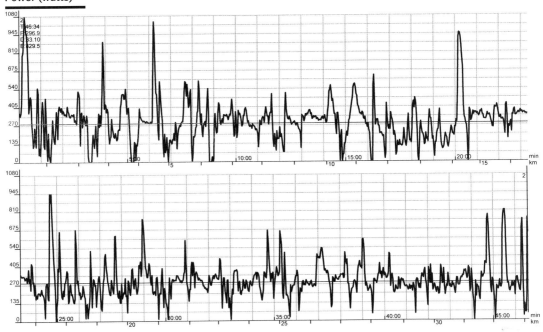

competition and seldom ranges more than 5 percent above or below the rider's MSPO. In fact, during the time trial this rider spent 89 percent of his time between 95 percent and 105 percent of his MSPO. In contrast, during the criterium he spent only 41 percent of his time between 95 percent and 105 percent of his MSPO. Also, notice that he spent about fifteen minutes in excess of 120 percent of his MSPO during the criterium, and only two minutes above this intensity during the time trial.

These graphs show the variation in power requirements for different events and illustrate the need to tailor a rider's training to her specific goals. Thus, riders who choose to focus on one type of event should have a training program that reflects the demands of that primary discipline. For instance, time trialing specialists should focus on workouts designed to increase their MSPO, while cyclists who wish to excel at stage racing would need to have a more rounded program to help them improve their ability to handle a wide variety of competitive situations.

only because the event is difficult and painful, but also because the training is so physically and mentally demanding. The positive side of training for time trials is that the conditioning and mental toughness you gain will help you in many other aspects of competitive cycling. A high MSPO is important for all endurance cyclists, and nowhere is it more vital than in time trials. Because of this need, training for time trials involves a large volume of SMSP and MSP intervals. Generally, these intervals are relatively short during the early part of the training program and stress a very high power output. As the training progresses, the work periods are lengthened and/or the rest periods shortened until the rider is able to maintain the desired power output for the entire length of a competitive event. The table on pages 102–3 provides a seven-week program designed to improve a rider's performance in a 20-kilometer time trial event. This rider has set a goal of completing the trial in twenty-four minutes and has determined, using a power meter, that he must be able to

Time Trialing

Time trials are particularly demanding because a rider must give a complete effort for the entire race. When competing in road races or criteriums, a cyclist has the opportunity to share the work with other riders and can rely on ingenuity as much as physical ability to win races. In contrast, time trials represent true tests of a cyclist's ability by requiring the most of his or her physical capacity, conditioning, and mental fortitude.

The time trial is the least-favorite event for many riders, not

Success in time trials requires a high maximum sustainable power output and the fortitude to endure pain.

SEVEN-WEEK IN-SEASON TRAINING PROGRAM FOR A TIME TRIALIST

	MONDAY	TUESDAY	WEDNES-DAY	THURSDAY	FRIDAY	SATURDAY	SUNDAY
WEEK 1	2 SETS, 3X 4 MIN. ON @ 385 WATTS, 4 MIN. BETW. REPS, 8 MIN. BETW. SETS	3 SETS, 4X 2 MIN. ON @ 400 WATTS, 90 SEC. BETW. REPS, 8 MIN. BETW. SETS	EASY/OFF	EASY/OFF	2 SETS, 3X 4 MIN. ON @ 385 WATTS, 3 MIN. BETW. REPS, 8 MIN. BETW. SETS	4 SETS, 2X 3 MIN. ON @ 395 WATTS, 90 SEC. BETW. REPS, 8 MIN. BETW. SETS	ROAD RACE
WEEK 2	EASY/OFF	EASY/OFF	1½ HR. IN ZONE 2	4X 6 MIN. ON @ 375 WATTS, 6 MIN. BETW. REPS	3 SETS, 4X 2 MIN. ON @ 410 WATTS, 1 MIN. BETW. REPS, 8 MIN. BETW. SETS	EASY/OFF	EASY/OFF
WEEK 3	2 SETS, 3X 4 MIN. ON @ 380 WATTS, 2 MIN. BETW. REPS, 8 MIN. BETW. SETS	3 SETS, 4X 2 MIN. ON @ 390 WATTS, 45 SEC. BETW. REPS, 6 MIN. BETW. SETS	EASY/OFF	EASY/OFF	4X 6 MIN. ON @ 375 WATTS, 4 MIN. BETW. REPS	TIME TRIAL, THEN 2 SETS, 4X 2 MIN. ON @ 385 WATTS, 30 SEC. BETW. REPS, 6 MIN. BETW. SETS	CRITERIUM OR ROAD RACE
WEEK 4	EASY/OFF	EASY/OFF	5X 1 MIN. ON @ 450 WATTS, 2 MIN. BETW. REPS	EASY/OFF	1 HR. IN ZONE 2	4X 6 MIN. ON @ 375 WATTS, 3 MIN. BETW. REPS	2 SETS, 3X 4 MIN. ON @ 370 WATTS, 1 MIN. BETW. REPS, 8 MIN. BETW. SETS

SEVEN-WEEK IN-SEASON TRAINING PROGRAM FOR A TIME TRIALIST (CONT.)

	MONDAY	TUESDAY	WEDNES-DAY	THURSDAY	FRIDAY	SATURDAY	SUNDAY
WEEK 5	EASY/OFF	EASY/OFF	3X 8 MIN. ON @ 370 WATTS, 4 MIN. BETW. REPS	2 SETS, 2X 6 MIN. ON @ 375 WATTS, 2 MIN. BETW. REPS, 8 MIN. BETW. SETS	EASY/OFF	EASY/OFF	2X 12 MIN. ON @ 365 WATTS, 6 MIN. BETW. REPS
WEEK 6	2 SETS, 2X 6 MIN. ON @ 375 WATTS, 1 MIN. BETW. REPS, 8 MIN. BETW. SETS	EASY/OFF	EASY/OFF	CLUB TIME TRIAL OR 2X 12 MIN. ON @ 365 WATTS, 4 MIN. BETW. REPS	3X 8 MIN. ON @ 375 WATTS, 3 MIN. BETW. REPS	EASY/OFF	EASY/OFF
WEEK 7	1 HR. IN ZONE 2	2 SETS, 2X 3 MIN. ON @ 400 WATTS, 1 MIN. BETW. REPS, 6 MIN. BETW. SETS	EASY/OFF	4X 2 MIN. ON @ 450 WATTS, 1 MIN. BETW. REPS	EASY/OFF	5X 1 MIN. ON @ 475 WATTS, 2 MIN. BETW. REPS	20-KM TIME TRIAL

maintain 350 watts for the duration of the race to accomplish this. A recent maximal steady state test has revealed his MSPO to be 330 watts. To gain the extra 20 watts at MSPO, the rider divides the twenty-four minutes of work into time intervals short enough for him to maintain at least 350 watts for the entire length of each interval. He then manipulates the length of the work and rest intervals until he achieves the training adaptations that allow him to produce 350 watts of power for twenty-four continuous minutes.

Criterium Racing

Criteriums place great demands on a rider's anaerobic ability, as they are largely characterized by very short, high-power efforts. Even during breakaways, long, sustained efforts are rare, as riders generally have to slow down to safely negotiate the corners. Thus, training for criteriums should focus primarily on sprinting and short, high-intensity intervals separated by incomplete recovery periods. The criterium rider's training also should not be without the longer intervals used to improve MSPO, as a high MSPO allows the rider to meet more of her energy demands without producing excessive amounts of lactic acid, thereby delaying the onset of muscular fatigue.

Thus, a criterium rider's training program should emphasize sprint and leadout intervals. Some longer SMSP intervals should also be incorporated to maintain a high MSPO. Long, slow endurance rides are kept to a minimum when training for criteriums, as they do nothing to increase a rider's sprinting ability, anaerobic capacity, and MSPO.

I frequently hear the argument that long, low-intensity rides are useful in preventing fatigue toward the end of criterium races. High-volume, low-intensity rides do increase the body's capacity to utilize fat as an energy source and can increase endurance capacity during low-intensity exercise. However, the physiological adaptations to high-volume, low-intensity training have no effect on the mechanisms that cause fatigue during short, high-intensity events like criteriums. Fatigue in criteriums is usually due to the cumulative effects of multiple, high-intensity efforts, which results in the buildup of hydrogen ions

(recall the role of hydrogen ions in muscular fatigue from chapter 2); riders who fatigue during the latter portions of criteriums are generally the victims of excessive production of lactic acid. Therefore, to counteract fatigue in criterium races, a cyclist should increase the volume of both leadout intervals, to enhance the body's ability to neutralize hydrogen ions, and SMSP intervals, to boost MSPO and reduce reliance on the anaerobic energy pathway.

A final note about training for criteriums. These races are typically held on technically difficult courses that demand much of your bike-handling ability. In fact, I have often seen races where riders who lack fitness are competitive simply because they possess superb bike-handling skills. Therefore, if you wish to excel in criteriums you should compete in these races regularly to develop and maintain these skills. Many cycling clubs put on midweek criterium races that you can use in place of an interval workout. If you do choose to take advantage of low-key club races to enhance your criterium skills, realize that you should make these races as

Large pelotons and technical courses require exceptional bike-handling skills from criterium racers.

THREE-WEEK IN-SEASON TRAINING PROGRAM FOR A CRITERIUM RACER

	MONDAY	TUESDAY	WEDNES-DAY	THURSDAY	FRIDAY	SATURDAY	SUNDAY
WEEK 1	SMSP INTERVALS: 2 SETS, 3X 4 MIN. ON, 4 MIN. OFF, 8 MIN. BETW. SETS	LEADOUT INTERVALS: 5 SETS, 5X 30 SEC. ON, 15 SEC. OFF, 3 MIN. BETW. SETS	1½ TO 2 HR. IN ZONE 2	EASY/OFF	SMSP INTERVALS: 5X 1 MIN. ON, 2 MIN. OFF	CRITERIUM	CRITERIUM
WEEK 2	EASY/OFF	SMSP INTERVALS: 4 SETS, 2X 3 MIN. ON, 1 MIN. OFF, 8 MIN. BETW. SETS	CLUB RACE OR LEADOUT INTERVALS: 6 SETS, 8X 20 SEC. ON, 10 SEC. OFF, 3 MIN. BETW. SETS	EASY/OFF	SMSP INTERVALS: 5X 1 MIN. ON, 2 MIN. OFF	CRITERIUM	CRITERIUM
WEEK 3	EASY/OFF	EASY/OFF	CLUB RACE OR LEADOUT INTERVALS: 6 SETS, 8X 20 SEC. ON, 10 SEC. OFF, 3 MIN. BETW. SETS	EASY/OFF	SMSP INTERVALS: 5X 1 MIN. ON, 2 MIN. OFF	CRITERIUM	CRITERIUM

difficult as possible by attacking aggressively and not hesitating to chase down others who have launched attacks of their own. Of course this strategy may decrease your chances of winning, but it will provide you with demanding training that will be helpful at more significant events.

Road Racing

Excelling in road racing requires more versatility than time trials or criteriums. The graph next page shows the power output of a cyclist during a four-hour road race. Notice the wide range of outputs. During the four hours of racing, this rider spent two hours and fifty minutes below his MSPO and almost an hour and ten minutes above it. Of the time spent above his MSPO, nearly fifty minutes was at 110 percent or more of his MSPO. The graph shows that many of these high power outputs came in short bursts of less than a minute, while other efforts were carried on for ten minutes or more. This graph clearly demonstrates that road races typically call on every ability in a cyclist's arsenal, ranging from several hours of low-intensity riding to some of the most intense sprinting imaginable. Thus, a road racer's training program needs to reflect the many requirements of these events, with special emphasis on the racer's weaknesses and the specialized demands of upcoming races. This means that a road racer will likely do several types of workouts during a training period.

While success in competitive road racing once again begins with a high MSPO, a cyclist must also develop other attributes. The ability to produce a high nonsustainable power output is necessary in situations such as instigating and chasing down breakaways and catching the peloton after a mechanical. Finally, the successful road racer must possess sprinting ability, as these races often turn on a sprint to the finish.

Formulating a training program that encompasses all the needs of a road racer can be a daunting task. However, it can be simplified if the rider uses a block training approach and remembers a few key rules.

1. Always arrange the workouts so that the most rigorous work is done at the beginning of the block and the least rigorous work at the end.

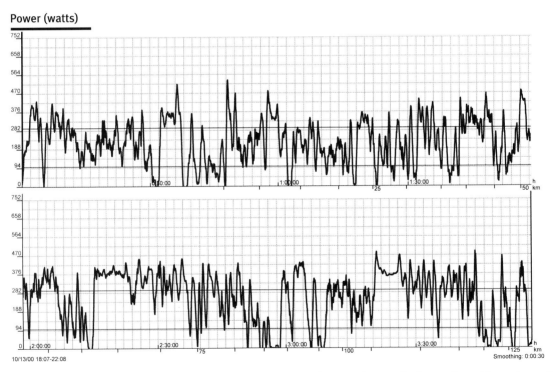

An SRM graph showing a rider's power output during a road race. The graph shows the wide variety of abilities necessary for success in road racing.

2. Recognize that the best approach may be to do two workouts on some training days.

3. Be willing to use weekend and club races as training, and remember that placing these races at the end of a training block can provide the necessary motivation to achieve good workouts.

4. Consume plenty of carbohydrate during these training blocks to ensure an adequate supply of glycogen (see chapter 10).

The table below shows a three-week training program for a cyclist who wishes to focus on road racing. Of course, the volume of the work-

THREE-WEEK IN-SEASON TRAINING PROGRAM FOR A ROAD RACER

	MONDAY	TUESDAY	WEDNES-DAY	THURSDAY	FRIDAY	SATURDAY	SUNDAY
WEEK 1	SMSP INTERVALS: 4X 4 MIN. ON, 4 MIN. OFF, 8 MIN. BETW. SETS	MSP INTERVALS: 3X 10 MIN. ON, 5 MIN. OFF (CLIMBING)	EASY/OFF	EASY/OFF	SMSP INTERVALS: 5X 1 MIN. ON, 2 MIN. OFF	RACE	RACE
WEEK 2	3 HR. IN ZONE 2	EASY/OFF	SPRINT INTERVALS: 2 SETS, 4X 15 SEC. ON, 90 SEC. OFF, 5 MIN. BETW. SETS	SMSP INTERVALS: 2 SETS, 5X 3 MIN. ON, 3 MIN. OFF, 8 MIN. BETW. SETS, OR CLUB CRITERIUM	EASY/OFF	RACE	RACE
WEEK 3	EASY/OFF	EASY/OFF	SMSP INTERVALS: 2 SETS, 5X 3 MIN. ON, 3 MIN. OFF, 8 MIN. BETW. SETS, OR CLUB CRITERIUM WITH LOTS OF SPRINTING	MSP INTERVALS: 3X 12 MIN. ON, 6 MIN. OFF (CLIMBING), OR CLUB TIME TRIAL	EASY/OFF	EASY/OFF	RACE

outs (both intervals and road rides) will depend on the racer's gender and racing category. The key is to recognize the demands of your chosen events and adjust your training to meet those demands. Notice the prominence of competitive group rides in this training schedule. Group rides can be very important workouts for the competitive road racer, because they typically encompass all of the requirements of road races and allow the rider to train each of these needs. Group rides also can make a racer aware of areas of weakness that should be addressed in specialized workouts. Finally, group rides can provide teams with opportunities to work together and practice race strategies. Remember, cycling is a team sport, and oftentimes the conditioning and ability of one rider cannot make up for a poorly organized team that does not execute a sound strategy.

Stage Racing

Like road racing, stage racing requires a wide variety of racing abilities. However, there are two basic differences between stage races and single-day road races that call for a change in training strategy. First and most obviously, stage races are run over multiple days, so riders must be conditioned to work very hard for several consecutive days. Second, despite their length, stage races usually feature just one or two key challenges or types of challenges that determine the winner for the entire race. Typically, the challenge is one or more time trials and/or long climbs. While good stage racers may rely heavily on their teammates to keep them in a race, it is generally their exceptional individual efforts during time trials or on demanding climbs that place them in a position to win the overall title. Thus, much like time trialing, training for stage racing involves considerable dedication to building MSPO. However, because the stage racer must also be competitive in pack-riding situations, long road races, and high-intensity criteriums, she or he must incorporate a bit more variation into training than the time trial specialist.

To build the stage racer's capacity to perform at high levels on consecutive days, training blocks are typically longer than those used

Although teamwork is important during stage racing, the winner of the race often is decided by exceptional individual effort.

by specialists in single-day events. Because long training blocks can be mentally taxing, often the best way to train is to include stage races as a regular part of the program. The competitive atmosphere of races can motivate the rider to perform consecutive days of hard training, so vital in preparing for stage rac-

ing. When stage races are not available, two or three days of hard training followed by a weekend of road or criterium racing can be an effective substitute.

Finally, unlike the training programs for road and criterium racers, there is little sprint work in the program for stage racers. This is

FIVE-WEEK IN-SEASON TRAINING PROGRAM FOR A STAGE RACER

	MONDAY	TUESDAY	WEDNES-DAY	THURSDAY	FRIDAY	SATURDAY	SUNDAY
WEEK 1	EASY/OFF	SMSP INTERVALS: 4 SETS, 3X 3 MIN. ON, 1 MIN. OFF, 10 MIN. BETW. SETS	CLUB RACE OR MSP INTERVALS: 4X 8 MIN. ON, 4 MIN. OFF (CLIMBING)	EASY/OFF	EASY/OFF	WEEKEND STAGE RACE	WEEKEND STAGE RACE
WEEK 2	4 HR. IN ZONE 2	EASY/OFF	EASY/OFF	SMSP INTERVALS: 2 SETS, 4X 4 MIN. ON, 4 MIN. OFF, 8 MIN. BETW. SETS	MSP INTERVALS: 5X 8 MIN. ON, 4 MIN. OFF	WEEKEND STAGE RACE	WEEKEND STAGE RACE
WEEK 3	EASY/OFF	EASY/OFF	EASY/OFF	SMSP INTERVALS: 2 SETS, 6X 1 MIN. ON, 2 MIN. OFF, 6 MIN. BETW. SETS, THEN 3 HR. IN ZONE 2	EASY/OFF	RACE	RACE

(continued next page)

FIVE-WEEK IN-SEASON TRAINING PROGRAM FOR A STAGE RACER (CONT.)

	MONDAY	TUESDAY	WEDNES-DAY	THURSDAY	FRIDAY	SATURDAY	SUNDAY
WEEK 4 (RECOVERY)	EASY/OFF	EASY/OFF	1 HR. IN ZONE 2	SMSP INTERVALS: 5X 1 MIN. ON, 2 MIN. OFF, THEN 1 HR. IN ZONE 2	EASY/OFF	CRITERIUM	EASY/OFF
WEEK 5 (COMPETITION)	1 HR. IN ZONE 2 WITH SMSP INTERVALS: 5X 1 MIN. ON, 2 MIN. OFF	STAGE RACE	STAGE RACE	STAGE RACE	STAGE RACE	STAGE RACE	STAGE RACE

because little if any time is gained in a sprint at the end of each individual stage. In fact, the person who wins the pack sprint at the end of a stage is sometimes given the same time as the last person to cross the finish line. Therefore, although sprinting ability is important in winning some individual stages, it generally has very little bearing on the overall winner of the race. Because of this, stage race specialists are better served by developing their MSPO rather than their sprinting ability. Furthermore, contenders for the overall win in a stage race are wise to let the sprinters fight for stage wins and save their energy for time trials and climbing stages, where they can gain several minutes on their competition.

Mountain Biking

Mountain bike races are similar to time trials in that a racer must rely on her or his individual effort to be successful. However, unlike most time trials where a relatively steady power output is maintained throughout, power output in mountain bike racing generally varies considerably with the uneven terrain of the race course. Despite this difference, mountain bikers, like time trialists, benefit greatly from a high MSPO. Anyone who doubts this should look at the development of Alison Dunlap, the 2001 World Cross Country Champion. Alison began her mountain biking career in 1997 after a long and decorated career as a road cyclist that included a silver medal in the team time trial event

Successful mountain bikers do a great deal of their preparation on the road bike. Here 2001 World Cross Country Champion Alison Dunlap competes in the Redlands Bicycle Classic.

at the 1993 World Championships and a spot on the 1996 Olympic Road Team. I was fortunate enough to meet and test Alison early in her career when I was working for the USOC, and over the years I have watched her develop into an exceptionally strong cyclist with a very high MSPO. Her development was due largely to her commitment to road cycling and her willingness to endure a high volume of very intense training. Because she established a high MSPO as a road cyclist, Alison's transition to competitive mountain biking was relatively smooth.

Despite her high MSPO, Alison's physiological development did require a bit of fine-tuning to make her the outstanding mountain

bike racer she is today. Her coach, Dean Golich, designed a training program specific to the demands of mountain biking. Dean had learned from data collected with the SRM that mountain bike racers normally face two main physiological challenges during competition: long, sustained efforts at or slightly above MSPO, typically encountered on long climbs; and shorter, higher-intensity efforts separated by incomplete recovery periods, typically found on courses over rolling terrain or on narrow, twisting trails.

Thus, like other competitive riders, mountain bike racers should take the time to raise their MSPO, which will improve their performance on long climbs and lessen their reliance on their anaerobic pathway for efforts above MSPO. After establishing a high MSPO, mountain bikers should increase their volume of short, high-intensity intervals to improve their ability to produce power during repeated, short efforts above MSPO. These intervals should be similar to the lead-out intervals described in chapter 6, but their length should vary from approximately twenty seconds to two minutes. Rest periods between the work intervals should range from one third to two thirds of the interval duration. Specific interval lengths and work to rest ratios will vary depending on a rider's development stage and the course characteristics of upcoming races.

I recommend that mountain bikers do the majority of their high-intensity work on the road bike. Training on the mountain bike over rugged terrain can impart a terrible pounding on the body, leaving the rider unable to perform the necessary volume of intervals or con-

THREE-WEEK IN-SEASON TRAINING PROGRAM FOR A MOUNTAIN BIKE RACER

	MONDAY	TUESDAY	WEDNES-DAY	THURSDAY	FRIDAY	SATURDAY	SUNDAY
WEEK 1	EASY/OFF	HARD CLUB RACE OR SMSP INTERVALS: 2 SETS, 4X 4 MIN. ON, 4 MIN. OFF, 8 MIN. BETW. SETS (ROAD BIKE)	2 HR. MOUNTAIN BIKE RIDE FOCUSING ON TECHNIQUE: DO AT LEAST 20 MIN. IN ZONE 5	EASY/OFF	EASY/OFF	EASY PRE-RIDE OF COURSE OR 1 HR. IN ZONE 2 WITH SMSP INTERVALS: 5X 1 MIN. ON, 2 MIN. OFF	MOUNTAIN BIKE RACE
WEEK 2	EASY/OFF	EASY/OFF	MSP INTERVALS: 4X 8 MIN. ON, 4 MIN. OFF (ON MOUNTAIN BIKE)	EASY/OFF	1 HR. IN ZONE 2 WITH SMSP INTERVALS: 5X 1 MIN. ON, 2 MIN. OFF	WEEKEND STAGE RACE	WEEKEND STAGE RACE
WEEK 3	EASY/OFF	EASY/OFF	HARD CLUB RACE OR SMSP INTERVALS: 2 SETS, 4X 4 MIN. ON, 4 MIN. OFF, 8 MIN. BETW. SETS (ON ROAD BIKE)	1 HR. EASY MOUNTAIN BIKE RIDE FOCUSING ON TECHNIQUE	EASY/OFF	EASY PRE-RIDE OF COURSE OR 1 HR. IN ZONE 2 WITH SMSP INTERVALS: 5X 1 MIN. ON, 2 MIN. OFF	MOUNTAIN BIKE RACE

Success in mountain bike racing requires excellent bike-handling skills.

secutive days of hard training. Doing workouts of similar intensity on the road requires less time for recovery and allows for a higher volume of high-intensity training. This is a tactic utilized by many of today's top off-road racers. In fact, the fields for many road and stage races often contain many of the world's top mountain bike racers.

As with criterium training, in-season training for mountain bike racing does not require frequent long, slow training rides, as race fatigue generally stems from the cumulative effects of repeated, high-intensity efforts. Therefore, mountain bikers who lack stamina will usually respond better to a training program that stresses more high-intensity intervals as opposed to long, low-intensity riding.

Finally, the mountain bike racer's training should include regular sessions devoted to bike handling. Race courses have become more technical as the sport has evolved, and excellent bike-handling skills are critical for success. In fact, I frequently see well-conditioned racers lose considerable time because of their inability to effectively negotiate technical sections of race courses.

The amount of time a rider needs to devote to bike handling will vary based on his or her ability. Mountain bike racers from BMX backgrounds usually possess excellent bike-handling skills and need very little work in this area. However, riders making the transition from road racing may need to initially spend two or three days a week developing their off-road skills.

Peaking for Specific Events

Peaking involves performing a progressive series of specialized workouts to meet the demands of a particular competition or series of events. Generally, these workouts begin several weeks in advance and become more specialized as the event draws nearer.

Once an athlete has selected an event, the first step in preparing for it is to understand its unique demands. The rider should identify the race course as soon as possible by, at the very least, obtaining a course profile and finding out about the expected weather conditions. If possible, riding the course several weeks before the competition can provide insight into how the race may unfold and where attacks are most likely to occur. Using a power meter while preriding the race course can provide additional information about the magnitude and type of power outputs that will be required.

The work I did for the U.S. national team in the mid-1990s provides a good example of using a power meter to determine the demands of competition. I was working with U.S. national team member Jane Quigley to help her prepare for the individual pursuit competition at the 1996 Olympic Trials. About six weeks before the competition I enlisted the help of then USOC biomechanist Jeff Broker to perform a test on the velodrome that would allow us to predict the power output Jane would need

to be in contention at the Olympic Trials. We outfitted Jane's pursuit bike with an SRM and had her ride on the velodrome at several different speeds. We then plotted each of her speeds against the corresponding power outputs and used a computer program to calculate the power she would need to generate to ride an individual pursuit at any given pace. I used that data to prescribe the proper training intensity for Jane's interval workouts. The result? Jane went to the Olympic Trials and, despite riding some very fast times, lost to the reigning World Champion Rebecca Twigg in the finals. However, later in the year Jane went on to win two World Cups and a silver medal in the points race at the World Championships. That year I also outfitted the bicycles of the men's pursuit team with SRMs to determine the power output required of each rider in each of the four positions of the competition. This allowed me to design more-specific workouts not only for the team as a whole, but also for each member.

Once a cyclist determines the requirements of a particular course, he or she can devise a training program for the event. The rider should begin this program after establishing an adequate fitness base, for example, by following the four-phase training program presented in chapter 7.

The length of a training period designed for peaking will vary substantially depending on the individual and the racing situation. It could be argued that an athlete who wishes to peak for an Olympic time trial may start training several years in advance by performing intervals to increase his or her MSPO. However, a truly specialized peaking program should last approximately eight weeks. This allows a rider two, three-week training periods separated by a four- to five-day recovery period and culminating with a seven- to ten-day taper prior to the competition.

Generally, a peaking period begins with

workouts that divide the demands of the competition into separate intervals. Initially, these intervals are relatively short and of an intensity that is higher than one could maintain for the duration of the competition. As the peaking period progresses, the length of the work intervals increases while exercise intensity remains steady, to provide training conditions that closely mimic the demands of competition. The peaking period ends with a seven- to ten-day taper in which training volume is significantly reduced while training intensity is maintained. Tapering allows the body to recover and supercompensate without losing its ability to work at high power outputs. The taper period culminates with a rest day two days before the competition and a low-volume, high-intensity workout the day before the competition.

When planning a specialized training program for peaking, don't lose sight of your goals. As I stated in chapter 4, winning or placing in a certain position in a particular event is not an appropriate goal for any rider. Therefore, do not confuse the act of peaking for an event with a long-term training plan designed to help you reach your goals as a cyclist. Remember that there are too many factors out of your control that can affect your competitive placement. However, your preparation is within your control, and by adhering to a specialized training program you can maximize your chances of winning a particular event.

Coaches frequently provide race support for their riders. Here, Barbara Blatter is encouraged by her coach, Gert-Jan Theunisse, at the 2001 Durango World Cup.

CHAPTER 9

Should You Hire a Coach?

As the sport of competitive cycling has grown, so has the demand for personal cycling coaches. Most athletes realize that simply going out and riding hard is not the optimal method for developing their abilities as cyclists, and many look for guidance from others. While a coach offers the competitive cyclist such benefits as race support, motivation, and information on training, one of the most important roles of a good coach is to provide objective advice about the athlete's training and development as a rider. Frequently, competitive cyclists get so caught up in the day-to-day responsibilities of training and racing that they don't plan more than a day in advance and don't remember more than a day in the past. As a result, they lose sight of their long-term goals, hindering their overall development. One job of a coach is to help you maintain the proper perspective on your overall training plan and to continually steer you in the right direction amid the distractions of long racing seasons.

Finding a good cycling coach is much more difficult than replying to an ad in a publication or on the Internet. You should not take the search lightly; the work you put into it is worth the effort. The search for the proper coach is a two-part process. First, you must recognize what you will need from your prospective coach. No coach is right for everyone, and your personality and needs as a rider will play a major role in your selection of the right coach from a group of eligible candidates. Second, you need to find a person who is qualified to meet your needs.

Evaluating Your Needs and Expectations

Before choosing a coach, ask yourself, "What do I really need from a coach?" Determining your needs as an athlete can have a great influence on whom you choose as a coach. For instance, if you have a degree in exercise physiology you are probably already able to devise an effective training program and may wish to look for a coach whose strengths include race strategy instead of training guidance. Other issues to consider include the following.

Motivation. Are you a self-motivated person, or do you require encouragement from an outside source to get the most out of your ability? If you depend on others for motivation, how dependent are you? Do you need an occasional push when times are tough or do you need constant encouragement?

Race support. Do you need someone to work the feed zone and provide you with tactical guidance?

Expense. Be realistic about how much you are willing to spend on a coach. Becoming a truly good coach takes an investment of time and money, so good coaches will generally cost more. However, what a coach charges may depend not only on his qualifications, but also on the amount of time and other resources you expect him to devote to you. For instance, if you want someone who will travel with you to races, you should expect to pay more than if you simply want a training program. Finally, for the majority of readers, bike racing is no more than a serious hobby. Very few of you will ever make a living racing a bicycle. Most of you recognize this and are willing to incur the expense of entry fees, travel, and equipment. To many coaches, however, competitive cycling is a way of life, and coaching is how they make their living. If riders are unwilling to pay a coach what he is worth, the coach will likely have to find another way to support himself, and then no one will get his help. Thus, don't expect a discount rate from a coach because you are a nice person or the fastest rider in your local club. Remember that good advice, like so many other good things, is expensive.

Evaluating a Potential Coach

Just because an individual rubs shoulders with successful riders, drops a few names in conversation, or has a fancy Web site does not make him a good coach. Throughout my ten years of coaching cyclists, I have seen plenty of incompetence and dishonesty even at the top levels of the profession. And although most approach their profession with the best of intentions, many coaches are woefully unprepared to provide sound advice on issues of training, nutrition, and race strategy. So check a

prospective coach's personal experience, educational background, and references to help you decide whether he is qualified to give you the guidance you need.

Competitive experience. One of the first issues you should consider when choosing a coach is his experience in competitive cycling. Is he familiar with the various requirements of bicycle racing? Does he understand the physical requirements of competition? Does he understand race strategy? Has he ever raced a bicycle and, if so, at what level? While professional cycling experience is certainly not a prerequisite for being a successful coach, some experience as a bicycle racer is helpful in understanding the requirements of the sport.

Education. Education in exercise physiology, the study of how the human body responds to exercise stress, can be extremely valuable in designing training programs. Unfortunately, most cycling coaches in the United States have very little formal education in this discipline and rely on their experience as former competitive cyclists to provide training guidance to their clients. Worse yet, some coaches seek advice from others who have no more knowledge about the topic than they do. While these coaches can provide valuable instruction about racing tactics, their lack of knowledge about exercise physiology can severely limit their ability to devise optimal training regimens. Furthermore, coaches who lack experience in performing and interpreting research will have a difficult time staying on the cutting edge of training techniques, and are more likely to provide their athletes with general programs from outside sources. In contrast, a coach with a solid background in exercise physiology will likely possess a better understanding of how the body responds to exercise training. This knowledge often means the coach is able to create innovative training programs that meet the specific needs of individual athletes.

Thus, finding a coach who understands the sport of bicycle racing and has an undergraduate degree in exercise physiology is great; if you can find one with a graduate degree in this area, even better.

Coaching certification. Unfortunately, certification programs for cycling coaches in the United States leave a great deal to be desired. While USA Cycling does offer a coaching certification program, some of its certification levels can be attained with only minimal knowledge. Formal education is cursory in the lower levels of USA Cycling's program and covers basic exercise physiology, nutrition, biomechanics, CPR, and coaching responsibilities. At the conclusion of instruction, students are given an unsupervised, open-book exam to assess their qualifications to be a coach. Thus, prospective coaches are able to consult their coaching manuals or confer with others while taking the test. This is hardly an adequate method to assess coaching knowledge and ability.

Communication. A coach should be a good communicator. This means that he should be able to explain clearly to you what you need to do and why. Call a prospective coach and dis-

The responsibilities of a cycling coach are far-ranging. Here, coach Des Dickie motorpaces national team athletes on the Colorado Springs Velodrome.

cuss your needs and his philosophy of training. Make note of how he proposes to address your needs and how well he answers your questions. This initial contact can give you an idea of how well you and the candidate would communicate in the coach-athlete relationship. Also, you should expect your phone calls and e-mails to be answered promptly and no question you pose to be left unanswered.

References. One way to assess a coach's ability is to look at the success of his riders. Generally, good coaches produce good riders.

However, don't be satisfied with a superficial observation of the coach's clients. Instead, ask the athletes what their coach has done for them. Ask questions like "Where were you before you got involved with your coach?" and "What has your coach done to help develop you as a rider?" Getting the answers to these questions can help you determine if a coach has been responsible for developing his clients into the cyclists they are or is simply fortunate enough to be involved with talented athletes.

Part Three

TRAINING AIDS

Consuming carbohydrate drinks during competition helps maintain hydration and energy levels.

CHAPTER 10

Ergogenic Aids

Ergogenic aids, agents that improve an individual's ability to do work, exist most commonly as nutritional supplements and pharmaceuticals. Caffeine, amphetamines, anabolic steroids, and a carbohydrate-rich diet are just a few examples. While many supplements found in the market are considered ergogenic, the vast majority of these provide benefits solely by the *placebo effect,* a change in performance or behavior resulting from the power of suggestion. In other words, if someone believes that consuming a particular product will improve performance, she or he may benefit from taking it. However, the benefit comes from believing a product will work and not from the product itself.

Evaluating Ergogenic Aids

Because bicycle racing is such a physically demanding sport, many cyclists turn to supplements in an attempt to improve performance. However, before you decide to plunk down money on the latest fad product, you should ask the following questions.

- Is the product legal?
- Is the product safe?
- Is the product effective?

The first issue is generally well defined, as the Union Cycliste Internationale (UCI) and the International Olympic Committee (IOC) have clear guidelines relating to the legality of many pharmaceutical and herbal supplements. Safety often goes hand in hand with legality, since many ergogenic aids are banned not only because they provide an unfair advantage, but also because their use may endanger the health of the athlete.

Unfortunately, determining the efficacy of an ergogenic aid is not always simple. While some agents are unquestionably effective, others have absolutely no ergogenic value at all. Still other substances are ergogenic in some situations but not in others. For instance, consuming a carbohydrate drink will certainly be ergogenic during a long road race, but not during a match sprint race.

The demand for ergogenic aids has created a multibillion-dollar industry that produces many products of questionable value. Frequently, shoddy research is performed or good research purposefully misinterpreted to provide scientific "proof" that is used to convince consumers to buy certain products. However, the term *proof* is often used inappropriately. Supplement manufacturers frequently use phrases such as "Research proves that our product is effective," when, in fact, research does not prove anything. Instead, research only provides data that either support or refute a claim. There is always the possibility, no matter how strong the data may be, that the conclusions reached by a researcher may be incorrect. Thus, you will rarely, if ever, hear a good scientist use the word *proof*, and when you see this word attached to a particular product, you should view that product with skepticism.

The prevalence of this junk science can make it difficult to determine the truth about many of the supplements on today's market. To truly test the efficacy of an ergogenic aid requires a combination of well-controlled laboratory and field experiments. This approach allows sports scientists to eliminate extraneous factors that may affect performance, leaving the researchers more assured that any change in performance is due to the agent.

The Importance of Statistical Significance

Even when research studies are properly designed and executed, the results can be manipulated to suggest something that isn't true. I have often seen instances where manufacturers claim that research demonstrated that their product improved performance, or improved performance by 10 percent, or 5 percent, etc. However, they often do not state whether this improvement was statistically significant. Many will argue that a 5 percent improvement in performance will, in all likelihood, improve a person's placement in a competitive event whether it is statistically significant or not. However, those who make this argument do not understand the meaning of the term *statistical significance*.

Typically, statistical significance is not determined to settle the argument over whether a particular level of improvement would make a difference in a competitive situation. Instead, statistics are used to determine if study data show a change in performance large and consistent enough to suggest that a particular product is actually effective. To illustrate this point, consider the following example.

A supplement manufacturer wishes to determine if a new product can improve time trial performance. To test this hypothesis, ten cyclists are recruited and each performs a 40-kilometer time trial. Five of the subjects are then assigned to receive the supplement and five are given a *placebo*. A placebo is an inert agent typically given to subjects in the control group of a research study. The placebo has no physiological effect and, because the subjects do not know whether they are receiving a placebo or an actual treatment, it eliminates the influence of the placebo effect. After three weeks of supplementation and training, the subjects repeat the 40-kilometer time trial. The data show that the group that took the supplement improved their time trial performance by an average of 5 percent while the placebo group shows no improvement. On the surface, it appears that the supplement is effective, and the manufacturer can honestly and rightfully claim that its product improved time trial performance by 5 percent in a scientific study. However, whether or not this 5 percent improvement in performance is statistically significant can determine if the product is truly ergogenic. For instance, if all five subjects showed a consistent increase in performance of 5 percent, then the results would be statistically significant and the new product could be considered truly ergogenic.

However, consider the following situation. After taking the supplement, one subject rides the time trial 30 percent faster than in the initial trial, a remarkable improvement. However, of the remaining four subjects, three show no improvement and the fourth rides 5 percent slower after supplementation. A quick calculation reveals that as a group, the subjects have still improved by an average of 5 percent, even though four of the five subjects showed no improvement or rode slower following supplementation!

Why did the fifth subject show such a marked improvement in performance? Considering that he was the only subject to exhibit such an effect, it is highly unlikely that his improvement was due to the supplement. Perhaps he was sick during the initial time trial, or he may have been a couch potato with no cycling experience prior to the study. Whatever the reason, the important point is that even though the group saw an average improvement of 5 percent, the improvements were not consistent enough among the subjects to be statistically significant. Thus, the product should not be considered ergogenic based on the results of the study.

Get the Whole Story

Consumers can be misled about a product's efficacy if they are not given all of the available information. In a recent book, the author cited a study by Nissen et al. to support his claim that beta-hydroxy beta-methylbutyrate (HMB) is an effective ergogenic aid. The author presented results showing that subjects who supplemented with HMB increased their lean body mass over the course of a three-week strength-training program more than those who did not consume HMB. The author also noted that total body strength increased following the strength-training program by 8 percent in subjects who did not supplement, compared to 13 percent and 18 percent in subjects who consumed 1.5 grams per day and 3.0 grams per day of HMB, respectively.

On the surface, these results appear to make a very strong case for HMB as an er-

gogenic aid. However, the author neglected to present all of the data from the study. First of all, while the average increase in lean body mass for subjects taking HMB was greater than for controls, this difference was small and not statistically significant. Furthermore, while Nissen et al. did see a significantly greater increase in total body strength in subjects who supplemented with HMB, only increases in lower body strength contributed to the differences between the groups. In other words, despite an equally rigorous lifting routine for the upper body, subjects who took HMB had no improvement in upper body strength. This leads to the question, if HMB is truly effective in improving muscular strength, why was it not effective in doing so for both the lower and upper body? Thus, consideration of all the data calls into question the efficacy of the product.

This is not to say that HMB may not eventually be accepted as an effective ergogenic aid, but it is clear that the jury is still out. However, in cases like this, fairness to the consumer dictates that all evidence, both positive and negative, be presented. This allows each individual to make an informed decision as to whether a product is worth the cost.

Conclusions Based on the Preponderance of Evidence

Unfortunately, even the best research cannot always separate effective ergogenic aids from ineffective ones. For a number of reasons, even scientific results cannot be relied upon as the absolute and final answer. First of all, scientists recognize that the results of even the best studies may be due to chance alone. Statistical approaches commonly used to analyze data allow scientists to be 95 percent confident that their conclusions are correct. In other words, in many research studies, there is a 5 percent chance that the conclusions are incorrect.

Proper selection of subjects is another factor that can affect the results of a research study. For instance, regular use of caffeine reduces an individual's sensitivity to its effects. Thus, tests of the ergogenic effects of caffeine should involve subjects who do not regularly consume caffeine. There is also the possibility that some research subjects are naturally more sensitive to a substance than others. So, while some subjects may exhibit a positive response to an experimental supplement, others may see little or no effect. Gender also plays a role in the proper selection of subjects. For instance, men and women have different needs for the element iron, so it would be inadvisable to generalize findings from a study on iron intake and male athletes to the iron needs of female athletes. Training status of subjects also may distort the results of a study, as athletes sometimes will react differently than untrained individuals to certain substances. Thus, results obtained from untrained subjects may not apply to athletic populations.

Another common mistake is making the assumption that people and animals respond identically to an experimental substance. I frequently see cases where supplement manufacturers point to studies conducted on animals to support claims that their products are ergogenic in humans. However, many agents can improve the work capacity of certain animal species but have no beneficial effects in humans.

The lesson to be learned is that you should not base your conclusions about a potential ergogenic aid on one study or on the claims of the manufacturer. Instead, examine reviews of several different studies performed by different research groups. You can then use the preponderance of the evidence to judge a supplement's benefits.

Reviews of Potential Ergogenic Agents

Below are reviews of some agents that have been touted as ergogenic aids. These reviews are based on data from a number of sources and, whenever possible, represent the latest information available. As you will see, some of the agents are effective at increasing work capacity, but the vast majority do not live up to the claims of being ergogenic. Still others may only be ergogenic in situations unlikely to be encountered by competitive cyclists. Should you decide to use a substance to improve your performance in a race, you are strongly advised to first experiment with it during training. This strategy will allow you to recognize any negative side effects before competition. Only agents deemed legal by the UCI and IOC are reviewed.

Coenzyme Q_{10}. Also known as *ubiquinone*, coenzyme Q_{10} is used by the body to make coenzyme Q, which catalyzes an energy-liberating step in the mitochondria. Advocates of supplementation speculate that consuming large amounts of ubiquinone will increase the level of coenzyme Q in the mitochondria and lead to greater energy availability. While research clearly demonstrates that supplementation with coenzyme Q_{10} does increase ubiquinone levels in the blood, supplementation appears to be ineffective in boosting the level of coenzyme Q in the mitochondria of healthy individuals. Furthermore, most research has found little if any effect on exercise performance. Ubiquinone supplementation has been shown to increase the work capacity of patients with heart disease and mitochondrial myopathy (a rare disease characterized by a gradual decrease in the size and number of mitochondria). Many supplement manufacturers use this evidence to claim that ubiquinone is an effective ergogenic aid; they just don't tell you that you have to be afflicted with one of these conditions to receive any benefit.

Ginseng. This substance, derived from the root of the Araliaceous plant, has been used in Asia for thousands of years to treat a wide variety of maladies ranging from excessive perspiration to tuberculosis. Interestingly, some practitioners of traditional Asian medicine claim that ginseng is both a sedative and a stimulant. Some research has demonstrated that consumption of ginseng can prolong time to exhaustion during exercise. However, the purity and concentration of the active ingredients in ginseng varies widely among marketed products, making it very difficult to recommend optimal dosages. Some positive effects on exercise capacity were noted following nine weeks of supplementing with 2×100 milligrams per day of Ginsana. Unfortunately, training during the supplementation period was poorly controlled. In fact, if there is one consistency among much of the research performed on ginseng, it is poor research methods. Thus, although some studies have indicated that ginseng has a positive effect on exercise performance, much work remains to be done in this area.

Ciwujia. Also known as *Siberian ginseng*, ciwujia is the active ingredient in the popular supplement known as Endurox (don't confuse this product with Endurox R^4, which does not contain ciwujia). The manufacturer of Endurox has produced a number of "scientific" studies to support its claims that the product can increase fat utilization and oxygen consumption and reduce blood lactate accumulation. However, the studies' research methods have not been disclosed to the greater scientific community. Furthermore, a number of independent laboratories have been unable to link ciwujia to any positive effects on fat utilization, oxygen consumption, blood lactate accumulation, or exercise performance. Thus, it does not appear that ciwujia can rightfully be called an ergogenic aid.

L-carnitine. The basis for carnitine supplementation lies with the enzyme carnitine acyl-transferase, which assists in the transport of fatty acids into the mitochondria of muscle cells, where they are burned for energy. Proponents of supplementation believe carnitine will increase carnitine acyl-transferase levels and ultimately increase fat utilization. As with other enzymes, the synthesis of carnitine acyl-transferase is stimulated by the increased need for the enzyme (as with exercise) and not the amount of excess carnitine available. Most research in this area has consistently failed to demonstrate a link between carnitine supplementation and carnitine acyl-transferase levels, increases in fatty acid utilization, or improvements in exercise performance.

Chromium picolinate. The element chromium assists insulin in transporting glucose and amino acids into muscle cells. When chromium levels are low, cells appear to be less sensitive to insulin. Thus, chromium supplementation has been proposed as a method for increasing glycogen storage and improving the capabilities for muscle repair and growth. Research, however, has yielded mixed results. Furthermore, there is no set RDA for chromium, as little is known about its minimum effective circulating levels. If you are considering chromium supplementation, be aware that recent research has demonstrated that excessive chromium intake has a negative effect on iron levels. When aged red blood cells have outlived their usefulness, they are destroyed and their iron is salvaged by transferrin. Chromium appears to compete with iron for the binding site on transferrin, reducing transferrin's ability to salvage iron and potentially leading to iron deficiency and anemia.

Phosphate. There are two ways in which phosphate loading may exert an ergogenic effect. First, it increases the availability of free phosphate in the muscle for creation of the high-energy compounds ATP and creatine phosphate. Second, increased phosphate levels increase levels of 2,3-diphosphoglycerate (2,3-DPG) in red blood cells, which reduces the red blood cells' affinity for oxygen, making it easier for oxygen to be transferred from the cells to working muscle.

Research on the ergogenic properties of phosphate loading has produced contradictory results. Some studies have observed increases in time to exhaustion during exercise, maximal oxygen consumption, and lactate threshold, while others have found no effect on exercise performance. Due to this scant and conflicting evidence, it is difficult to make definitive recommendations about its use. However, studies that have shown benefits from phosphate loading have used a loading technique that involves consuming 4 to 6 grams of *sodium* phosphate per day for three to four days. After supplementation, phosphate levels in the body remain elevated for about two weeks, so the loading process must be repeated regularly to continue to enjoy benefits.

Note that phosphate is generally available in two forms, sodium phosphate and calcium phosphate. While some studies have shown positive effects from loading with sodium phosphate, research on calcium phosphate has thus far demonstrated no ergogenic effects. Finally, if you do choose to use sodium phosphate, be forewarned that oral consumption can cause gastric distress (stomachache) and that chronic supplementation can result in calcium deficiency.

Phosphatidylserine. The interest in phosphatidylserine as an ergogenic aid centers on its ability to suppress the release of the hormone cortisol. Secreted by the adrenal cortex in response to physical and emotional stress, cortisol breaks down glycogen and proteins to provide energy to the working muscle. Following exercise, cortisol levels remain elevated for several hours, assisting in recovery by mobilizing proteins for repair of damaged muscle fibers. However, because cortisol acts to break down muscle proteins, it must be absent before the muscle-building phase of recovery can take place, or the damaged muscle fibers would be torn down as quickly as they were repaired. Thus, while cortisol levels rise during and immediately following intense exercise, they typically return to lower levels within a few hours, allowing recovery to proceed.

Due to the degenerative effects of chronically elevated cortisol levels on muscle tissue, some researchers have wondered about a possible link between cortisol and overtraining. Indeed, some athletes who are beginning to have difficulty responding to and performing normal training do show elevated resting levels of cortisol. This possible relationship suggests that phosphatidylserine may be effective in preventing or treating symptoms of overtraining.

Unfortunately, however, the link between cortisol and overtraining is not well understood. Some individuals with symptoms of overtraining have normal or lowered blood cortisol levels. Furthermore, because of the vital role cortisol plays in mobilizing energy substrates during exercise and in instigating recovery following exercise, constant suppression of cortisol may ultimately prove detrimental. Finally, although phosphatidylserine holds promise, to date no published research has demonstrated that it can be used to prevent or treat symptoms of overtraining or improve performance.

Beta-hydroxy beta-methylbutyrate (HMB). Some time ago, researchers noticed that when samples of muscle tissue were placed in a solution containing HMB, muscle protein degradation was inhibited. This led to speculation that HMB could reduce exercise-induced muscle damage, increase muscle mass, and improve exercise performance. While most research has shown an association between HMB supplementation and a reduction in physiological markers of exercise-induced muscle damage, the effects of HMB on lean body mass (muscle) and exercise performance are less clear. Several investigations have suggested that HMB supplementation can lead to increased lean body mass and improved strength, but others have failed to find any significant changes in these parameters. Further adding to the confusion, some studies have produced results that both support and refute the effectiveness of HMB. For instance, in the study discussed on page 125, subjects who supplemented with HMB while participating in a resistance training program increased their lower body strength but not their upper body strength. Yet another investigation noted an increase in lean body mass in individuals who supplemented with 3 grams per day of HMB, but a decrease in lean body mass in those who consumed 6 grams per day.

Although research continues, definitive recommendations about HMB usage cannot yet be made. However, it does appear that supplementation with 1.5 to 3 grams per day of HMB is safe and may help lessen exercise-induced muscle damage, increase muscle mass, and improve exercise performance.

Leucine, isoleucine, valine. These amino acids are commonly referred to as *branched-chain amino acids* (BCAAs) because of their chemical structures. BCAAs have been shown to stimulate protein synthesis and reduce protein degradation; they are also associated with mobilizing amino acids for use as an energy source. Although research has demonstrated that heavy exercise can result in decreased blood and muscular levels of BCAAs, this has not been linked to a decrease in exercise performance. It also is unclear whether long-term BCAA supplementation can improve exercise performance or response to training. On a positive note, one study observed a glycogen-sparing effect when subjects consumed 90 milligrams per kilogram of body weight of BCAAs before and during exhaustive endurance exercise. Unfortunately, this study did not measure exercise performance. Despite this positive finding, the usefulness of BCAAs is still in question, as several researchers have found that consuming carbohydrates before and during exercise better preserves muscle glycogen than consuming branched-chain amino acids. Furthermore, research has demonstrated that consuming BCAAs in addition to carbohydrates is no more effective in sparing muscle glycogen and improving performance than consuming carbohydrates alone.

If you choose to supplement with BCAAs, be aware that their absorption from the gut depends on carriers that transport amino acids across the intestinal wall. These carriers are not specific for any particular amino acid, and when faced with a high concentration of one amino acid they will transport greater amounts of it. This can result in an artificial shortage of other amino acids that compete for the same carrier. To avoid this problem, take amino acid supplements between meals or as part of a post-workout recovery drink.

Echinacea. This herbal supplement may be able to bolster the immune system of the upper respiratory tract, where viral infections that cause the common cold take hold. The research is still in its early stages, and though the evidence is not plentiful, it is promising. It is prudent to begin with very small quantities of echinacea, as it can cause an allergic reaction in some people. Eventual effective dosages appear to be in the area of 1 to 2 grams per day. Be forewarned, however, that there is suspicion among health professionals that long-term supplementation with echinacea may suppress the body's natural production of immuno-bodies, leaving users susceptible to infection when they stop supplementation. Because of this, I would not recommend taking echinacea for more than eight to ten days in a row. Using the product at key times such as during stressful situations or during training camps when you are around more people (and thus more viruses) than usual could prove to be an effective practice.

Medium-chain triglycerides (MCTs). These fats are moderately sized triglyceride molecules. Being fats, MCTs provide a calorically dense fuel for the body, but without compromising gastric emptying and absorption rates commonly seen with consumption of larger triglycerides. Although MCTs cannot provide fuel for high-intensity efforts, they do appear to be able to reduce the body's reliance on glycogen during low- to moderate-intensity exercise. Because high-intensity exercise is fueled almost entirely by carbohydrate, the MCTs' glycogen-sparing effect can allow a rider to perform a higher volume of high-intensity work before glycogen stores become depleted.

Other Potential Ergogenic Aids

Carbohydrate

Carbohydrate, consumed in adequate amounts, is probably the most consistently effective ergogenic aid available to the endurance athlete. Fatigue in endurance events is highly correlated with muscle glycogen depletion. Athletes who take part in competitions and training sessions that are excessively long or repeated on consecutive days are at risk for muscle glycogen depletion. Combining a carbohydrate-rich diet with carbohydrate consumption prior to and/or during endurance exercise

helps maintain glycogen levels and can improve performance.

How Much Carbohydrate Is Needed?

Dietary carbohydrate consumption can be divided into two categories. Basic carbohydrate consumption consists of carbohydrates consumed as a regular part of meals or snacks, while event-specific carbohydrate consumption consists of those consumed as part of the pre-event meal, during the exercise event, and immediately after exercise.

Traditionally, recommended carbohydrate intake for cyclists has been expressed as a percentage of total calories. Endurance athletes are usually urged to consume approximately 60 to 70 percent of their total daily caloric intake as carbohydrate. However, calorie consumption varies widely among athletes, so this formula may leave some individuals lacking in carbohydrates. Recent research investigating the absolute amount of carbohydrate required to maintain glycogen stores suggests that endurance athletes should consume approximately 6 to 10 grams of carbohydrate per kilogram of body weight per day, depending on the volume and intensity of their training. Consuming greater amounts does not seem to be of any benefit: when humans are fed more than 10 grams per kilogram per day, glycogen stores do not show further increases.

The timing of carbohydrate consumption also can significantly affect exercise performance. Providing 5 grams of carbohydrate per kilogram of body weight (about 350 grams for a 150-pound person) four hours before exercise has been shown to significantly improve endurance exercise performance. Likewise, cyclists who consume 40 to 60 grams of carbohydrate per hour (about one to one and a half 20-ounce bottles of commercially available sports drinks containing 6 to 9 percent carbohydrate) during exercise increase their time to exhaustion compared with trials in which they do not consume carbohydrate. Notably, researchers have found that when carbohydrate ingestion before exercise and during exercise are combined, performance is improved to a greater extent than when either strategy is used alone.

Carbohydrate consumption during the hours following an event can be equally important. It has been demonstrated that physiological changes take place during exercise that increase the rate at which carbohydrate can enter muscle cells. These conditions persist for several hours after the end of exercise, but are most prevalent during the first thirty to forty-five minutes after exercise. As would be expected, research has shown that athletes who consume large amounts of carbohydrate within forty-five minutes after the cessation of exercise maintain higher muscle glycogen levels than those who consume the same amount of carbohydrate at evenly spaced intervals during the day. Therefore, endurance athletes should consume 1.25 grams of carbohydrate per kilogram of body weight within thirty to forty-five minutes after the cessation of exercise and 1 gram per kilogram of body weight every two hours for six hours after a workout to aid in replenishing glycogen stores.

What Type of Carbohydrate Should Be Consumed?

For basic carbohydrate consumption, an athlete should consume a variety of complex carbohydrate such as breads, cereals, fruits, and pasta. Foods rich in complex carbohydrate are often rich in other necessary nutrients as well. In contrast, many foods high in simple carbohydrate do not offer a wide variety of other nutrients.

Event-specific carbohydrate consumption should be restricted to specific types of carbohydrate, as the type of carbohydrate consumed prior to, during, and following an event can exert significant effects on performance. These carbohydrates should be of the type that are quickly absorbed, do not cause gastric distress, and have a pleasing taste. Glucose, fructose, and sucrose (sugar formed by combining glucose and fructose) are the three most popular of these carbohydrate types.

Of these three sugars, glucose has several qualities that make it a superior energy source. The first is the way it is absorbed from the intestine into the bloodstream. Within the wall of the intestine are glucose carriers that assist in the transport of glucose from the gut into the bloodstream. No such carriers exist for fructose, which slows its rate of absorption. As for sucrose, it is broken down into its constituents and absorbed as glucose and fructose. Because of its carriers, glucose generally is absorbed more quickly than fructose, providing a significant advantage during exercise as well as after exercise, when muscle glycogen is being restored. In fact, when 0.7 gram per kilogram of body weight of glucose or sucrose is provided immediately following and at two-hour intervals after exercise, the rate of muscle glycogen resynthesis is double that when equal amounts of fructose are provided. Furthermore, when glucose is transported across the wall of the small intestine by a glucose transporter, water is drawn across with it. Therefore, water that is mixed with glucose is absorbed more quickly than water by itself or in a water-fructose mixture, which helps in maintaining proper hydration.

Once these sugars are absorbed into the bloodstream, they are transported to the liver and then released into the general circulation, where they can be transported to the working muscle. However, because all sugars must be converted into glucose before being released from the liver, fructose encounters further delays before it can provide glucose to muscle.

Therefore, glucose would appear to be the carbohydrate of choice, especially during exercise. However, the taste of sports drinks and other carbohydrate supplements influences their effectiveness. Research has demonstrated that when athletes like the taste of a sports drink, they consume more of it, which significantly improves its effectiveness. Glucose is not as sweet as fructose or sucrose, and a drink composed of only glucose is generally not very pleasing to the palate. Therefore, many sports drinks include at least some fructose or sucrose to improve their taste. However, because of the difficulties in digesting and metabolizing fructose, you should avoid drink mixes that list fructose as the first ingredient.

Dosage summary

You'll need 6 to 10 grams of carbohydrate per kilogram of body weight per day, including the following supplementation.

- 5 grams per kilogram of body weight three to four hours before competitive events or long training rides
- 40 to 60 grams (20 to 30 ounces of properly mixed carbohydrate drink or one to one and a half 20-ounce water bottles) per hour during exercise
- 1.25 grams per kilogram of body weight immediately following and 1 gram per kilogram of body weight every two hours for six hours after exercising for an hour or more (meals are included in this amount).

APPROXIMATE CARBOHYDRATE DOSAGES BASED ON BODY WEIGHT

BODY WEIGHT (lb.)	CARBOHYDRATE (g/kg of body weight)							
	1	1.25	5	6	7	8	9	10
100	45	57	227	273	318	364	409	455
110	50	63	250	300	350	400	450	500
120	55	68	273	327	382	436	491	545
130	59	74	295	355	414	473	532	591
140	64	80	318	382	445	509	573	636
150	68	85	341	409	477	545	614	682
160	73	91	364	436	509	582	655	727
170	77	97	386	464	541	618	695	773
180	82	102	409	491	573	655	736	818
190	86	108	432	518	605	691	777	864
200	91	114	455	545	636	727	818	909

To determine your weight in kilograms, divide your weight in pounds by 2.2. Then, to determine your total carbohydrate need, multiply your weight in kilograms by the recommended carbohydrate intakes. The table opposite provides approximate values.

Caffeine

Two purported physiological effects of caffeine have led to its widespread use as an ergogenic aid. First, caffeine has been shown to increase the twitch speed and strength of contracting muscle fibers under certain conditions. Second, it has been shown to increase endurance capacity by mobilizing fat for use as fuel by the working muscle.

Effects on Muscle Twitch Speed and Strength

The evidence that caffeine consumption increases contractile speed and strength is not very decisive. Scientists have demonstrated that caffeine can increase muscular strength and twitch speed using a variety of in vitro research techniques. These are studies that involve removing muscle samples from the body and exposing them to solutions containing high concentrations of caffeine. The muscle samples are then stimulated and their force production and twitch speed measured.

Unfortunately, the concentrations required to consistently elicit these ergogenic effects in the test tube are quite high and could not be attained by consuming caffeine without making an individual severely ill. Thus, while some studies have shown that caffeine can improve muscular strength and performance in short, high-intensity events, the majority of research has not corroborated this.

Effects on Endurance Exercise Performance

Endurance exercise performance is limited by levels of muscle glycogen (stored carbohydrate). Overwhelming evidence suggests that depletion of muscle glycogen results in the inability to perform all but the lowest intensity of exercise. Because of muscle glycogen's importance, much research in exercise physiology has focused on methods of maintaining it during prolonged exercise. The most successful method by far that we know of to preserve muscle glycogen is the consumption of carbohydrate prior to and during competition. However, over the last decade research has suggested that caffeine also may serve this purpose during exercise.

The proposed mechanism by which caffeine spares muscle glycogen is by increasing the availability of fats to be burned for energy. In many studies, consumption of approximately 4 to 9 milligrams of caffeine per kilogram of body weight one to three hours prior to exercise increased the blood level of free fatty acids (FFAs) and decreased the rate of muscle glycogen utilization during the early stages of exercise. However, after fifteen to thirty minutes of continuous exercise, the body begins to naturally mobilize FFAs to a degree equal to that induced by caffeine. Thus, the rate of muscle glycogen expenditure after the initial fifteen to thirty minutes of exercise does not appear to be affected by the consumption of caffeine. Nevertheless, using caffeine to spare muscle glycogen in the early stages of exercise has been shown to prolong time to exhaustion during low- to moderate-intensity exercise.

Despite a large and growing body of evidence that caffeine can prolong time to exhaustion in endurance exercise, its practical usefulness during competition is less clear for two reasons. First, the consumption of carbohydrate appears to reduce the metabolic effects and eliminate the ergogenic effects of caffeine. Studies investigating the combined effects of caffeine and carbohydrate have generally shown that the combination has no more effect on exercise performance than carbohydrate alone. Therefore, because of the effectiveness and widespread use of carbohydrate, caffeine may be unnecessary. Second, most studies demonstrating caffeine's ergogenic effect have required subjects to exercise to exhaustion at constant, subthreshold work rates. In contrast, success in most cycling events is measured by the amount of time it takes an athlete to cover a given distance, and research on caffeine's effect on this aspect of performance has produced conflicting results.

To examine the effects of caffeine in competitive situations, a 1979 study by Dr. John Ivy and Dr. David Costill had trained cyclists perform as much work as possible during a two-hour time trial while consuming placebo, carbohydrate drink, or caffeine. The subjects performed significantly more work during the caffeine trial than during the placebo or carbohydrate trials. However, since that time numerous studies designed to simulate competitive situations have failed to demonstrate an ergogenic effect for caffeine. Furthermore, the majority of the evidence continues to suggest that consuming carbohydrate prior to and during exercise is more effective than consuming caffeine in increasing exercise performance.

Why the conflicting evidence? A possible answer is provided by Dr. Costill, of Ball State University. Costill, who is one of the most prolific researchers in the field of exercise physiology, suggests that individual variations in subjects' responses to caffeine may seriously affect study results. Furthermore, he says that his early work, which demonstrated caffeine's

ergogenic effect, may not be representative of the effects of caffeine on the general population. Costill used many of the same subjects for each of his early studies, and considering the conflicting data from later studies, he now wonders if his early results were simply a consequence of having a group of subjects who were highly sensitive to caffeine. Finally, according to Costill, individual sensitivity to caffeine may be one of the most important factors in one's ability to respond to caffeine supplementation.

Practical Applications

Research has demonstrated that caffeine is most effective as an ergogenic aid in events where glycogen depletion is an issue. During longer events, caffeine's effects appear to be influenced by an individual's reaction to caffeine ingestion. Although caffeine's efficacy as an ergogenic aid is in question, moderate consumption is relatively safe. However, when taken in large amounts, caffeine may result in insomnia, irritability, anxiety, diarrhea, nausea, and heart arrhythmia.

Supplemental Strategies

Due to the IOC's position of allowing caffeine consumption in limited amounts, athletes may be confused as to how much to consume to receive the ergogenic benefits without facing disqualification. Typically, consumption of at least 5 to 6 milligrams of caffeine per kilogram of body weight has been required to elicit an ergogenic effect. Dosages of 9 milligrams per kilogram of caffeine have resulted in urinary concentrations of caffeine beyond the legal limit of 12 micrograms per milliliter. Therefore, a 70-kilogram cyclist should consume at least 350 milligrams but no more than 560 milligrams of caffeine to receive benefits but still remain within legal limits. Be aware that a number of sports drinks, gels, energy bars, and over-the-counter pain relievers contain caffeine, and consumption of these products in addition to caffeine supplementation may place you at risk of exceeding the legal limit.

Timing of caffeine ingestion also is important. Research indicates that blood levels of FFAs peak about three hours after caffeine ingestion, which should coincide with the start of exercise. Caffeine should be consumed in a single dose three hours prior to the start of an event. The glycogen-sparing effect of caffeine is eliminated after the first thirty minutes of exercise, so consumption of caffeine during an event is probably of no benefit. Because regular use of caffeine can reduce your sensitivity to its effects, you should refrain from caffeine consumption for at least seventy-two hours prior to an event in which you will use caffeine. Finally, as with all ergogenic aids, use caffeine in practice before an event to detect any possible side effects.

Sodium Bicarbonate

Glycolysis is the primary energy pathway for maximal or near-maximal exercise lasting longer than twenty to thirty seconds. Continued glycolysis results in a buildup of hydrogen ions in the muscle tissue, which eventually inhibits muscular contraction and glycolysis (see chapter 2). To slow their accumulation in the muscle, hydrogen ions are transported into the blood, where they can be neutralized by bases found there (acid + base = neutral). The rate of the transfer of hydrogen ions is influenced by the acid-base gradient between the muscle and the blood; in other words, the more basic the blood, the faster the hydrogen ions will flow out of the muscle and be neutralized. Consumption of sodium bicarbonate (a base) has been shown to increase the basic component

of the blood and increase its power to neutralize hydrogen ions, thus counteracting their detrimental effects.

Practical Applications

Research indicates that the effectiveness of sodium bicarbonate depends on the length and intensity of the activity, the dose of the supplement, and when it was taken. Sodium bicarbonate has the greatest effect on single events lasting one to seven minutes or repeated, high-intensity work intervals of one minute or less. Events such as individual and team pursuit, points race, miss and out, and possibly the kilometer are probably the best candidates for bicarbonate ingestion. The effective dose appears to be at least 0.3 gram per kilogram of body weight taken over a short time period one and a half hours before exercise.

Other Considerations

Sodium bicarbonate doses necessary to elicit an ergogenic effect are also associated with gastric distress and diarrhea. While in many cases these effects are unavoidable, you may reduce the immediate stomach discomfort if you accompany the sodium bicarbonate with large amounts of water (about 1.5 liters). Due to the great possibility of these side effects, if you are considering using sodium bicarbonate during competition you are *strongly* advised to experiment with recommended doses during training. If you tolerate the dosages, you can feel comfortable about using *that dosage* during competition. You should *never* consume experimental dosages during competition.

A second consideration is training status. Research indicates that sodium bicarbonate is most effective in highly anaerobic events lasting at least one to seven minutes. However, most research has used untrained or endurance-trained individuals as subjects. Anaerobic training increases an individual's natural ability to buffer hydrogen ions, and the small amount of research using anaerobically trained athletes suggests that sodium bicarbonate is less effective or ineffective in improving their performance. Again, the best course of action is to experiment with sodium bicarbonate in training or even in a laboratory assessment. If you attain no or only a slight ergogenic benefit, you may not find it worthwhile to use sodium bicarbonate during competition.

Finally, extensive use of sodium bicarbonate during training is not currently recommended. A major adaptation of anaerobic training is an increase of the body's natural buffering capability. By artificially increasing this capacity during training, you reduce the body's need to respond with its own buffering mechanism and may compromise training-induced increases in buffering capacity. However, more research is needed in this area before specific recommendations can be made.

Glycerol

Prolonged exercise, especially in warm environments, can result in dehydration. While severe fluid loss compromises the body's thermoregulatory process and can eventually result in death, even mild dehydration can impair exercise performance. Glycerol is a hydrophilic (water-attracting) compound that occurs naturally in the body. Recently, researchers have demonstrated that consumption of glycerol in combination with large volumes of water can increase water retention, delay dehydration, and improve exercise performance in hot environments.

In a study conducted at the University of New Mexico, cyclists were able to ride significantly longer in exercise trials preceded by the consumption of glycerol and water than in trials in which they consumed only water. Another study performed at the Australian Institute of Sport compared performance in 30-minute time trials following consumption of glycerol and water versus plain water. The results showed that when subjects consumed glycerol and water they were able to ride at a higher power output and perform more work during the time trial than when they consumed only water.

Most successful hydration strategies utilizing glycerol involve consuming about 1 gram of glycerol per kilogram of body weight along with 25 milliliters of water per kilogram of body weight (there are about 30 milliliters in an ounce and about 600 milliliters in a 20-ounce water bottle). Thus, a 150-pound (68-kilogram) rider would require about 68 grams of glycerol and approximately 1,700 milliliters of water, which amounts to about three 20-ounce water bottles. These should be consumed over a period of a half hour or so and finished about two hours before the start of the race.

If you choose to use glycerol, be aware that it is not without its pitfalls. Because of its attraction to water, glycerol consumed in large amounts has been shown to draw water out of the central nervous system, resulting in headaches and dizziness. Thus, it is a good idea to experiment before using glycerol in competition.

Dosage summary
- determine your glycerol dosage: 1 gram of glycerol per kilogram of body weight
- determine your water dosage: 25 milliliters of water per kilogram of body weight
- mix the water and glycerol and drink the mixture two to three hours before competition

Creatine

Creatine has been shown to be an effective ergogenic aid under very specific circumstances, but if proper dosages are not used or the product is used inappropriately, it is completely useless. Creatine in the form of creatine phosphate (CP) is an important substrate in the metabolic pathways that supply energy to working muscle. Energy for a muscular contraction is supplied by cleaving a phosphate from adenosine triphosphate (ATP) by the reaction: $ATP \rightarrow ADP + P_i + energy$. Bodily stores of ATP are very limited, and depletion has been shown to contribute to fatigue; therefore, they must be constantly replenished to maintain work capacity.

Recall from chapter 2 that CP can be used to regenerate ATP by donating its phosphate to an ADP molecule: $CP + ADP \rightarrow ATP + creatine$. This reaction can regenerate ATP supplies very quickly and is the primary pathway utilized during short, high-intensity efforts such as sprinting. Unfortunately, CP stores are very limited and are themselves depleted within a few seconds of the onset of strenuous exercise. This provides the basis for creatine supplementation.

The creatine necessary for the production of CP can be synthesized by the body from amino acids or supplied via dietary sources such as meat. It has been theorized that supplementation with creatine can increase bodily stores of creatine and therefore, considering that free phosphate is quite plentiful, increase CP levels. Numerous studies have shown that proper creatine supplementation can significantly increase bodily creatine stores in some people. Unfortunately, in none of these studies have the rises in creatine significantly increased resting CP levels. Since creatine must be combined with free phosphate to form CP before it can be used to replenish ATP, it would seem that creatine supplementation would not be useful as an ergogenic aid.

All is not be lost, however; it appears that increasing creatine stores may be useful in accelerating recovery rates during interval workouts. During recovery periods of reduced intensity or complete rest, CP is regenerated by the reaction: creatine + phosphate $\rightarrow$ creatine phosphate. This is a *substrate-limiting reaction*, which means that its rate is regulated by the concentration of the substrates (creatine and phosphate). Because phosphate is generally available in unlimited amounts, it will not be a limiting factor in the rate of CP resynthesis. Creatine, on the other hand, is in relatively limited supply. Thus, increasing the amount of creatine available can speed the rate of the reaction and restore effective levels of CP more quickly (see graph next page). The end result is a decrease in the time required for an individual to recover from short, intense work periods.

With creatine supplementation, it appears that the rate of CP resynthesis does not increase until after approximately two minutes of recovery. Research has also demonstrated that CP levels can be completely restored within eight to ten minutes after being depleted by severe exercise. Therefore, rest periods during interval sessions utilizing short, high-intensity work periods should be at least two minutes long for creatine supplementation to impart any benefit, but need not be longer than eight to ten minutes to restore CP levels.

Effects of Creatine Supplementation on Performance

Research measuring the ergogenic effect of creatine supplementation on different types of exercise has produced mixed results. As may be expected, the greatest benefits are seen in exercise regimens employing strenuous intervals separated by rest periods. However, even in these types of workouts, increasing bodily creatine stores does not seem to increase the ability to do work until late in the workout, after the subject has already completed several intervals (when recovery becomes more important).

CP Resynthesis Rate

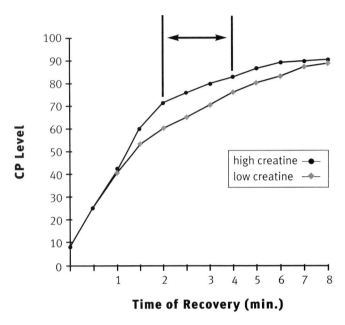

The effect of creatine supplementation on creatine phosphate (CP) synthesis during recovery. The arrow indicates the time period during which creatine supplementation resulted in a significantly faster rate of CP synthesis.

separated by periods of rest lasting at least two minutes. Events such as cross-country mountain biking, the miss and out, and the points race appear to be prime candidates for creatine supplementation. High-intensity events such as the match sprint, individual and team pursuit, and the kilometer lack the necessary recovery periods to make increased creatine levels beneficial, and recovery time between races generally allows complete restoration of CP stores. Therefore, creatine supplementation would probably not directly benefit performance in these events. However, because training for these types of events often involves high-intensity, interval-type workouts, creatine supplementation during these training periods may improve workout quality, resulting in an athlete who is better prepared for competition.

Creatine supplementation has never demonstrated effectiveness in single-effort, maximal-intensity events, presumably because of the lack of a recovery period to allow for the replenishment of CP stores. Likewise, creatine does not appear to enhance performance in long, endurance exercise events. In fact, one study found that after supplementing with creatine, trained distance runners ran significantly slower over a rolling, four-mile course than after supplementing with a placebo.

Practical Applications

Creatine supplementation appears to be beneficial only in activities that feature short (less than forty-five seconds), high-intensity efforts

Supplementation Strategies

A well-conceived supplementation strategy is essential to raising bodily creatine stores. Once creatine is ingested and absorbed into the bloodstream, it must be transported into the muscle to be effective. Supplementation with 5 grams of creatine four times per day for seven to ten days has been shown to significantly increase creatine levels in the blood and muscle. Studies have demonstrated that insulin may assist in transporting creatine into the muscle, so it may help to consume creatine with a high-carbohydrate meal (which will stimulate insulin release). The transport of substrates is also facilitated during and for two to three hours after exercise. Because of the synergistic effect of exercise and insulin on substrate transport, consuming creatine after exercise along with carbohydrate replenishment drinks may improve uptake of creatine by the muscle.

Little work has been done to determine how long after a bout of creatine supplementation bodily creatine levels will remain elevated. Therefore, any advice about dosages required for creatine maintenance would be purely speculative. However, it would seem prudent to consume a lower dose of creatine (approximately 2 grams four times per day) after the original supplementation period for the duration of the high-intensity interval training period.

A possible side effect of supplementation may arise from the fact that enzymes controlling creatine synthesis are reduced when creatine levels are high, so creatine supplementation may decrease the body's ability to form creatine. Therefore, take extreme care when terminating creatine supplementation and reduce the supplements gradually over a period of several days to avoid deficiencies.

Finally, despite promising results in studies of creatine supplementation, individual reactions to the consumption of creatine vary. Some individuals may see large increases in creatine levels and others little or no increase while undergoing identical supplementation regimens.

Dosage summary

Creatine is useful in any event or training situation that utilizes repeated, short (thirty to forty-five seconds), intense efforts separated by recovery periods of two to four minutes; this includes weightlifting. Doses should be taken approximately every four hours and preferably either with a high-carbohydrate meal or within two hours after a workout.

- initial: 5 grams of creatine four times a day for ten days before an event or interval-training period

- maintenance: 2 grams of creatine four times per day for the duration of the event or training period
- taper: after the event or training period, gradually reduce the creatine dosage over the following two weeks until no creatine is being consumed

Altitude Training and Alternatives

Training in high-altitude environments has been a popular ergogenic aid since the 1968 Olympic Games in Mexico City. The decreased availability of oxygen at high altitudes prompts the body to secrete the hormone erythropoietin (EPO), which stimulates production of red blood cells and increases their numbers in the bloodstream. This adaptation increases the blood's oxygen-carrying capacity, helping to maintain the delivery of oxygen to the working muscle.

There is ample evidence of improvements in exercise performance at sea level when red blood cell numbers are artificially enhanced by the administration of EPO and *blood doping,* a process where red blood cells are infused directly into the blood. The success of these techniques has prompted athletes and coaches to use altitude exposure to enhance the red blood cell response and improve exercise performance at sea level.

In spite of the widespread belief in altitude training among athletes and coaches, scientific research has consistently failed to find any benefit to sea-level performance. While some studies have shown ergogenic effects, most of these results can be traced to statistical anomalies or poor research methods. This lack of scientific support for altitude training has led some coaches and athletes to dismiss scientists as "ivory tower elitists" who are out of touch with the real world. However, by better understanding physiological adaptations to altitude training, coaches, athletes, and scientists can gain insight into the discrepancies between the anecdotal claims of athletes and the research data of scientists. Learning more about these adaptations may also help athletes determine if altitude exposure can help them.

Although increasing circulating red blood cell numbers is clearly ergogenic, other issues involved with altitude training can cause a significant drop in exercise performance, especially during the first few weeks of altitude exposure. Most obviously, the reduction in oxygen availability reduces aerobic capacity. While EPO production does begin almost immediately upon arrival at altitude, the subsequent increase in red blood cell numbers can take several weeks and may not be complete for several months. During this time, an athlete's aerobic power is compromised and she or he is required to rely more heavily on the anaerobic energy system to maintain exercise intensity. However, anaerobic capacity is also compromised during the early phases of altitude exposure. Adaptation to high-altitude environments involves a reduction in blood levels of bicarbonate (a basic compound used to help maintain the acid-base balance in the blood by neutralizing hydrogen ions), reducing the body's ability to tolerate the hydrogen ions that result from the production and decay of lactic acid. While this loss of buffering capacity does not typically hinder single, short, high-intensity efforts, the ability to perform repeated or lengthy high-intensity efforts is reduced. Thus, during the first several weeks at altitude, an athlete's ability to maintain training intensity is significantly compromised, and usually offsets the major benefit of altitude exposure—an increase in red blood cell numbers.

Once the athlete returns to sea level, training intensity can be restored. Many coaches and athletes argue that during this brief post-

exposure period, the increase in oxygen delivery to the working muscle should allow the athlete to increase his or her training intensity and experience an enhanced training effect. However, before taking advantage of the increase in red blood cells to improve performance beyond pre-exposure levels, the athlete must first overcome the effects of detraining caused by altitude exposure. Considering that red blood cell numbers remain elevated for only a couple of weeks after the return to sea level, it is very difficult to make any true gains from altitude training. Of course, athletes do *feel* better after returning from altitude, but this could be analogous to hitting yourself on the head with a hammer—it just feels better once you stop doing it.

This is not to say that altitude training is completely without its uses. Exposure to altitude during training periods that do not stress high-intensity intervals is one strategy that can potentially enhance performance. For example, conducting the weightlifting and high-volume, low-intensity training phases at high altitude would allow red blood cell numbers to increase but have minimum impact on high-intensity interval training. With the cyclist's ability to delivery oxygen to the working muscle at its peak, she could then return to sea level to perform SMSP intervals.

Duration of exposure and elevation are two other important factors in planning trips to high altitudes. Traditional strategies involve exposure periods of approximately three weeks at altitudes of 7,000 to 9,000 feet. However, scientific evidence suggests that this approach may result in only minimal increases in red blood cell numbers. While altitude exposures of three weeks are popular among many coaches and athletes, they typically do not result in large increases in red blood cells unless conducted at 12,000 feet or higher. Unfortunately, exposure to such extreme elevations can result in a number of side effects, so athletes seeking suitable environments for altitude training should stay in the range of 7,000 to 9,000 feet. However, because of the weaker EPO response at these altitudes, cyclists should consider extending their stays to as long as eight weeks.

Altitude training can also help prepare athletes for competitions held at altitude. Prior exposure and acclimation to the competitive environment can enhance competitive performance at altitude. Although optimum strategies have not been determined, athletes appear to respond well to single exposures of six to eight weeks or multiple exposures of two to three weeks at an elevation similar to that of competition. Ideally, the timing of these exposures should minimize disruptions to high-intensity training.

For athletes who are unable to incorporate altitude exposure into their preparation for high-altitude competition, the timing of their arrival before competition is critical. Evidence suggests that unacclimated athletes perform better within two to three days of their arrival than after two to three weeks of exposure to altitude. This is likely due to the cumulative stress brought on by altitude exposure over time, which causes unacclimated cyclists to become progressively fatigued. Furthermore, some researchers have observed a decrease in blood flow to working muscle during trips to high altitude, but not until the eighth day of exposure; blood flow during the initial week of exposure appeared normal.

If you do decide to incorporate altitude exposures into your training, or must compete at altitude, be sure you are properly prepared to meet the challenges of high-altitude environments by following these guidelines.

Drink plenty of water upon arrival. The atmosphere at altitude is typically more arid than at sea level. The lower humidity combined with an increase in respiration hastens dehydration.

Use sunscreen and sunglasses. Ultraviolet light is far more prevalent at altitude due to the decreased filtering capacity of the atmosphere. Thus, you are more susceptible to sunburn during altitude exposures.

Be prepared for abrupt weather changes. Weather patterns at altitude are variable and can change abruptly. I recall a mountain bike ride I took in the foothills around Colorado Springs one early autumn day. The temperature was in the mid-seventies and I rode in shorts and a sleeveless jersey. Two hours after my ride, a cold front passed through the area; the temperature dropped about forty degrees and it began to snow. The following day the temperature never rose out of the thirties. These types of changes are not unusual in high-altitude environments, so you should be prepared for any type of weather.

Be prepared for nighttime sleep disturbances. Difficulty in sleeping through the night is common, especially during the early days of altitude exposure. In severe cases, lack of adequate sleep can disrupt training. If this happens to you, consider using an over-the-counter sleeping aid such as diphenhydramine or incorporating afternoon naps into your schedule.

Consider taking a blood test. Several weeks before leaving for altitude, take a blood test to evaluate your iron status. Some researchers have noted that individuals with iron deficiencies are unable to make significant gains in red blood cell numbers in response to altitude exposure. A simple blood test, taken four to six weeks before leaving for altitude, and subsequent supplementation (if warranted) will ensure that your iron levels are adequate for new red blood cell production.

Consider the length of your exposure. Your altitude exposure should last at least three weeks, and you should consider longer exposures (up to eight weeks).

Stay at elevations of approximately 7,000 to 9,000 feet. Lower elevations are less effective in stimulating increases in red blood cell numbers, especially during short (three-week) sojourns. Exposure to elevations higher than 9,000 feet seems to increase the likelihood and severity of the negative effects of altitude exposure.

Sea-level training zones won't apply. Your power outputs during intervals at and above maximal steady state will be lower at altitude. Your exercising heart rate will also be affected: maximal heart rate is reduced while heart rates at any given submaximal work rate are higher than at sea level.

Time your trips. Plan your altitude exposures so they do not occur during periods of high-intensity training.

Avoid altitude exposure during the final preparation period for sea-level competitions. The side effects will likely cancel out any benefits you gain from increased red blood cell production.

Intermittent Hypoxia Training

In the late 1980s and early 1990s, physiologists began experimenting with a novel training approach in which athletes lived and/or slept in high-altitude environments and trained at significantly lower altitudes. The rationale was that this would allow athletes to gain the benefits of altitude exposure while avoiding the reduction in training intensity and subsequent detraining commonly experienced during altitude training.

In a landmark investigation, Dr. Ben Levine and Dr. Jim Stray-Gundersen studied the performance of three groups of competitive runners who underwent four-week training regimens. All three groups followed a similar training program, but did so in three different environments. One group lived and trained at sea level, a second lived and trained at 2,500 meters (about 8,200 feet), while the third lived at 2,500 meters but was transported each day to an elevation of 1,250 meters for training. Following the four-week training program, only the groups exposed to altitude saw significant increases in red blood cell numbers. However, the group that trained at 1,250 meters was able to perform their running intervals at a significantly higher intensity than those who remained at 2,500 meters. In fact, only the group that trained at 2,500 meters saw a significant reduction in training intensity when compared to sea-level exercise performance. Finally, following the four-week training program, only the group that lived at 2,500 meters and trained at 1,250 meters saw a significant improvement in their performance in a 5,000-meter run at sea level. This study provides strong evidence that altitude exposure may be useful only when it does not compromise training intensity.

Entrepreneurs have capitalized on these findings by developing altitude tents that use oxygen dilution techniques to simulate high altitudes. This technology, known as *intermittent hypoxia training*, allows athletes to sleep in relatively high-altitude environments and train at lower altitudes. While very little research has been performed on the effects of intermittent hypoxia on red blood cell numbers and competitive performance, most researchers agree that this method has great potential as an ergogenic aid. Currently, not enough is known about intermittent hypoxia to make definitive recommendations about optimum sleeping elevations or exposure durations. However, most researchers agree that the optimum dosage of intermittent hypoxia will depend on the degree of hypoxia and the frequency and duration of exposures.

Hyperoxic Training

Since I have lived in Colorado Springs and worked as a physiologist for the USOC and USA Cycling, I have focused on developing better training methods for athletes. One area of particular interest to me and the other physiologists at the USOC was how to develop a live high–train low approach that could take advantage of the natural high-altitude environment of Colorado Springs. Thousands of elite athletes travel to the U.S. Olympic Training Center every year for training camps, and hundreds more who are part of the USOC's resident program live in Colorado Springs for much of the year. To help these athletes optimize their training, we considered several approaches to increase training intensity in Colorado's high elevations.

In 1995, in an attempt to solve this problem, I directed a study of the effects of breathing hyperoxic (oxygen-rich) gas on training intensity and exercise performance. We recruited competitive cyclists from sea-level environments and brought them to the high-altitude environment of Colorado Springs. Over a three-week period, half of the subjects performed nine interval training sessions while breathing normal air, and the other half performed identical intervals while breathing a hyperoxic mixture of gas that simulated sea-level conditions.

The results showed that subjects who breathed the hyperoxic mixture were able to train at higher power outputs than those who breathed the normal air. Furthermore, the subjects who used the oxygen-enriched air significantly improved their maximal steady state power output and their time trial performance, while the other group showed no improvements in these areas.

Since the initial study in 1995, several top cyclists and other athletes have utilized hyperoxic training. Alison Dunlap, Mari Holden, Jane Quigley, Mike Creed, and Sarah Hammer have all incorporated this technique into their training plans. Outside the cycling world, hyperoxic training was used by the U.S. Long Track Speed Skating Team in their preparation for the 2002 Olympic Games. Their results in Salt Lake City were nothing short of extraordinary, and their coaches acknowledged that the team performed well beyond their most optimistic expectations.

I am continuing to study the effects of hyperoxic training on cycling performance. In a recent study, we investigated the effects of breathing hyperoxic gas on the performance of long-term

Sarah Hammer performs intervals while breathing 60 percent oxygen. Normal air contains only 21 percent oxygen. The higher oxygen level allows her to increase her power output by 10 percent and results in a superior training effect.

high-altitude residents. Our findings showed that breathing a mixture containing 60 percent oxygen increased the training power outputs of these subjects by 10 percent. Similar increases in power outputs have been observed in individuals who live at sea level when they breathed hyperoxic gas during high-intensity intervals. These results suggest that hyperoxic training is not only beneficial during altitude training, but can improve exercise performance in many other situations as well.

Administering hyperoxic gases to an exercising athlete requires elaborate equipment and trained technicians. Currently, hyperoxic training is not available to the general public, and unless you are part of a national team in a sport associated with the USOC your chances of getting to use it are rather slim. However, I have been consulting with a group that is interested in building equipment that would allow anyone to utilize hyperoxic training. The group plans to have a product on the market by late 2003 or early 2004 at a cost that is comparable to a good racing bicycle.

Questions and Answers

Q. How do I determine if a particular sports drink contains the proper concentration of carbohydrate?
A. First, we need to divide sports drinks into two categories: those consumed during workouts or competitions, and those consumed before or after exercise. For those consumed during exercise, the carbohydrate concentrations should be in the range of 6 to 9 percent. Higher concentrations reduce the rate of digestion and can slow the absorption of water from the gut, which can result in dehydration. To determine the carbohydrate concentration of any beverage, look at the label on the package. Among other things, the label will list the serving size (typically 8 ounces, or 240 milliliters) and the amount of carbohydrate (in grams) per serving. To calculate the carbohydrate concentration, divide the amount of carbohydrate in grams by the serving size in milliliters. For instance, a sports drink that contains 15 grams of carbohydrate in a 240-milliliter serving would contain $15 \div 240 = 0.06$, or 6 percent carbohydrate.

As for pre- or postexercise drinks, the rate of carbohydrate delivery to the muscle takes precedence over fluid absorption. Thus, the carbohydrate concentrations of these drinks can be considerably higher.

Q. I drink Coke during races and training rides for the carbohydrate and the caffeine. Is this a good strategy?
A. While it is a good idea to consume carbohydrate during races and long training rides, drinking caffeinated soda is not the best way to do this for two reasons. First, sodas primarily use fructose as their sweetener. Compared to glucose or sucrose, fructose slows the rates of digestion and delivery of glucose to the working muscle. Second, the carbohydrate concentrations in soda are high (about 13 percent; those in sports drinks are generally 6 to 9 percent), which also slows the rate of digestion. As for the caffeine, a beverage like Coke contains 75 milligrams in a 20-ounce bottle, well below the level required for an ergogenic effect. Furthermore, the ideal time to consume caffeine is one to three hours before an event, so a small amount of caffeine during exercise probably has minimal, if any, effect on performance.

Q. I prefer to eat cookies or fruit as opposed to energy bars or gels during my rides. Is this OK?
A. While common snacks like cookies and fruit can be tasty alternatives to products designed to be eaten during exercise, they do have their drawbacks. Fruits are typically high in fructose

and fiber, both of which slow the rates of digestion and glucose delivery to the muscle. Cookies, in addition to being high in carbohydrate, are usually high in fat as well. While fat can supply energy for exercise, it typically slows the rate of digestion.

Q. Doesn't the use of caffeine promote dehydration?
A. Caffeine is a diuretic, and the increase in urinary volume can promote dehydration. However, this diuretic effect seems to be eliminated during exercise. So, if consuming caffeine before an event increases your need to use the bathroom, just continue to hydrate prior to the event and, once the race begins, you should be fine. As with all ergogenic aids, it is wise to try out a substance while training before using it in competition. In the case of caffeine, this strategy will help you balance your increased urinary output with an increase in fluid intake prior to an event.

Directions for the Future

Much of the "new" information presented in this book has been known to scientists for a number of years, but most of it has not been presented to cyclists in usable form. Other information, particularly about block training and power-based workouts, is the result of relatively new discoveries in the scientific study of cyclists and bicycle racing. Much of this research has been possible due to advances in power meters. Recent innovations in these devices have brought science and competitive cycling closer together than ever before. When I first saw the Powerscan in the human performance laboratory at the U.S. Olympic Training Center in 1992, I knew this kind of instrument had the potential to change the sport of competitive bicycle racing forever. Because of power meters, sports scientists now have a better understanding of the demands of competitive cycling, and cyclists are better able to incorporate scientific information into their training programs.

How will the nature of athletic training and preparation change in the future? The most likely source of tomorrow's innovations will be the field of genetics. The qualities of the human body are, to a great extent, controlled by the approximately thirty thousand genes that make up the human genome. Each one of these genes is responsible for producing a specific protein, among them proteins important for exercise performance. These include proteins that are used to create muscle tissue or make the enzymes that drive the reactions in the energy pathways, as well as hormones like testosterone, insulin, and erythropoietin. Exercise training stimulates the genes to produce more of these proteins, and this helps athletes improve their performance. Thus, one of the future challenges for sports scientists will be to identify the genes that play vital roles in exercise performance and learn how to stimulate them to produce their proteins. This, however, is the topic of another story.

References

Chapter 1

Alway, S. E. 1994. Force and contractile characteristics after stretch overload in quail anterior latissimus dorsi muscle. *Journal of Applied Physiology* 77(1): 135–141.

Andersen, J. L., H. Klitgaard, and B. Saltin. 1994. Myosin heavy chain isoforms in single fibres from m. vastus lateralis of sprinters: influence of training. *Acta Physiologica Scandinavica* 155: 135–142.

Åstrand, P. O., and K. Rodahl. 1986. *Textbook of Work Physiology,* 3rd ed. New York: McGraw-Hill.

Awede, B., et al. 1999. Adaptations of mouse skeletal muscle to novel functional overload test: changes in myosin heavy chains and SERCA and physiological consequences. *European Journal of Applied Physiology* 80: 519–526.

Esbjörnsson, M., et al. 1993. Muscle fibre type changes with sprint training: effect of training pattern. *Acta Physiologica Scandinavica* 149: 245–246.

Essig, D. A., et al. 1990. Acceleration of myosin heavy chain isoform transitions during compensatory hypertrophy of developing avian muscles. In Taylor, A. W., and P. D. Gollnick (Eds.), *Biochemistry of Exercise VII.* Champaign, IL: Human Kinetics.

Gray, A. B., R. D. Telford, and M. J. Weidmann. 1993. Endocrine response to intense interval exercise. *European Journal of Applied Physiology* 66: 366–371.

Green, H. J., et al. 1984. Exercise-induced fibre type transitions with regard to myosin, parvalbumin, and sarcoplasmic reticulum in muscles of the rat. *Pflügers Archives* 400: 432–438.

Green, H. J., et al. 1992. Metabolite patterns related to exhaustion, recovery and transformation of chronically stimulated rabbit fast-twitch muscle. *European Journal of Applied Physiology* 420: 359–366.

Guyton, A. C. 1986. *Textbook of Medical Physiology,* 7th ed. Philadelphia: W.B. Saunders.

Hoogeveen, A. R., and M. L. Zonderland. 1996. Relationships between testosterone, cortisol and performance in professional cyclists. *International Journal of Sports Medicine* 17(6): 423–428.

Hunt, T. K., and M. Z. Hussain. 1994. Can wound healing be a paradigm for tissue repair? *Medicine and Science in Sports and Exercise* 26(6): 755–758.

Jurime, J., et al. 1996. Changes in myosin heavy chain isoform profile of the triceps brachii muscle following 12 weeks of resistance training. *European Journal of Applied Physiology* 74(3): 287–292.

Mazzeo, R. F. 1991. Catecholamine responses to acute and chronic exercise. *Medicine and Science in Sports and Exercise* 23(7): 839–845.

Mikesky, A. E., et al. 1991. Changes in muscle fiber size and composition in response to heavy-resistance exercise. *Medicine and Science in Sports and Exercise* 23(9): 1042–1049.

Oishi, Y., H. Yamamoto, and E. Miyamoto. 1994. Changes in fiber-type composition and myosin heavy-chain IId isoform in rat soleus muscle during recovery period after hindlimb suspension. *European Journal of Applied Physiology* 68(1): 102–106.

Roman, W. J., and S. E. Alway. 1995. Stretch-induced transformations in myosin expression of quail anterior latissimus dorsi muscle. *Medicine and Science in Sports and Exercise* 27(11): 1494–1499.

Schiaffino, S., and C. Reggiani. 1994. Myosin isoforms in mammalian skeletal muscle. *Journal of Applied Physiology* 77(2): 493–501.

Staron, R. S. 1997. Human skeletal muscle fiber types: delineation, development, and distribution. *Canadian Journal of Applied Physiology* 22(4): 307–327.

Timson, B. F. 1990. Evaluation of animal models for the study of exercise-induced muscle enlargement. *Journal of Applied Physiology* 69(6): 1935–1945.

Timson, B. F., et al. 1985. Fiber number, area, and composition of mouse soleus muscle following enlargement. *Journal of Applied Physiology* 58(2): 619–624.

Vasankari, T. J., et al. 1993. Effects of endurance training on hormonal responses to prolonged physical exercise in males. *Acta Endocrinologica* 129: 109–113.

Williamson, D. L., et al. 2001. Reduction in hybrid single muscle fiber proportions with resistance training in humans. *Journal of Applied Physiology* 91: 1955–1961.

Chapter 2

Aunola, S., and H. Rusko. 1992. Does anaerobic threshold correlate with maximal lactate steady state? *Journal of Sports Sciences* 10: 309–323.

Bowtell, J. L., et al. 1999. Effects of oral glutamine on whole body carbohydrate storage during recovery from exhaustive exercise. *Journal of Applied Physiology* 86(6): 1770–1777.

Bowtell, J. L., et al. 2000. Effect of different carbohydrate drinks on whole body carbohydrate storage after exercise. *Journal of Applied Physiology* 88: 1529–1536.

Brooks, G. A. 1985. Anaerobic threshold: review of the concept and directions for future research. *Medicine and Science in Sports and Exercise* 17(1): 22–31.

Brooks, G. A. 1986. The lactate shuttle during exercise and recovery. *Medicine and Science in Sports and Exercise* 18(3): 360–368.

Brooks, G. A. 1987. Amino acids and protein metabolism during exercise and recovery. *Medicine and Science in Sports and Exercise* 19(5): S150–S156.

Brooks, G. A. 1991. Current concepts in lactate exchange. *Medicine and Science in Sports and Exercise* 23(8): 895–906.

Brooks, G. A., and T. D. Fahey. 1984. *Exercise Physiology: Human Bioenergetics and Its Applications.* New York: Macmillan.

Brouns, F., et al. 1989. Eating, drinking, and cycling. A controlled Tour de France simulation study, part I. *International Journal of Sports Medicine* 10: S32–S40.

Brouns, F., et al. 1989. Metabolic changes induced by sustained exhaustive cycling and diet manipulations. *International Journal of Sports Medicine* 10: S49–S62.

Brown, R. C., C. M. Cox, and A. Goulding. 2000. High-carbohydrate versus high-fat diets: effect on body composition in trained cyclists. *Medicine and Science in Sports and Exercise* 32(3): 690–694.

Coggan, A. R., and S. C. Swanson. 1992. Nutritional manipulations before and during endurance exercise: effects on performance. *Medicine and Science in Sports and Exercise* 24(9): S331–S335.

Davis, J. M., et al. 1999. Effects of branched-chain amino acids and carbohydrate on fatigue during intermittent, high-intensity running. *International Journal of Sports Medicine* 20: 309–314.

Dekkers, J. C., L. P. J. van Doornen, and H. C. G. Kemper. 1996. The role of antioxidant vitamins and enzymes in the prevention of exercise induced muscle damage. *Sports Medicine* 21(3): 213–238.

Febbraio, M. A., and J. Dancey. 1999. Skeletal muscle energy metabolism during prolonged, fatiguing exercise. *Journal of Applied Physiology* 87(6): 2341–2347.

Febbraio, M. A., and K. L. Stewart. 1996. CHO feeding before prolonged exercise: effect of glycemic index on muscle glycogenolysis and exercise performance. *Journal of Applied Physiology* 81(2): 1115–1120.

Forslund, A. H., et al. 1998. The 24-h whole body leucine and urea kinetics at normal and high protein intakes with exercise in healthy adults. *Journal of Applied Physiology* 275: E310–E320.

Horton, T. J., et al. 1995. Fat and carbohydrate overfeeding in humans: different effects on energy storage. *American Journal of Clinical Nutrition* 62: 19–29.

Ivy, J. L., et al. 1979. Influence of caffeine and carbohydrate feedings on endurance performance. *Medicine and Science in Sports and Exercise* 11(1): 6–11.

Ivy, J. L., et al. 1988. Muscle glycogen synthesis after exercise: effect of time of carbohydrate ingestion. *Journal of Applied Physiology* 64(4): 1480–1485.

Katz, A., and K. Sahlin. 1988. Regulation of lactic acid production during exercise. *Journal of Applied Physiology* 65(2): 509–518.

Keizer, H. A., et al. 1986. Influence of liquid and solid meals on muscle glycogen resynthesis, plasma fuel hormone response, and maximal physical working capacity. *International Journal of Sports Medicine* 8(2): 99–104.

Kemp, G. J., et al. 1997. Proton efflux in human skeletal muscle during recovery from exercise. *European Journal of Applied Physiology* 76: 462–471.

LaFontaine, T. P., B. R. Londeree, and W. K. Spath. 1981. The maximal steady state versus

selected running events. *Medicine and Science in Sports and Exercise* 13(3): 190–192.

Lehninger, A. L. 1979. *Biochemistry: The Molecular Basis of Cell Structure and Function*, 2d ed. New York: Worth Publishers.

Londeree, B. R., and S. A. Ames. 1975. Maximal steady state versus state of conditioning. *European Journal of Applied Physiology* 34: 269–278.

McConell, G., K. Kloot, and M. Hargreaves. 1996. Effect of timing of carbohydrate ingestion on endurance performance. *Medicine and Science in Sports and Exercise* 28(10): 1300–1304.

Meredith, C. N., et al. 1989. Dietary protein requirements and body protein metabolism in endurance-trained men. *Journal of Applied Physiology* 66(6): 2850–2856.

Mittendorfer, B., and L. S. Sidossis. 2001. Mechanism for the increase in plasma triacylglycerol concentrations after consumption of short-term, high-carbohydrate diets. *American Journal of Clinical Nutrition* 73: 892–899.

Paul, G. L. 1989. Dietary protein requirements of physically active individuals. *Sports Medicine* 8(3): 154–176.

Quiron, A., et al. 1988. Lactate threshold and onset of blood lactate accumulation during incremental exercise after dietary modifications. *European Journal of Applied Physiology* 57: 192–197.

Ranallo, R. F., and E. C. Rhodes. 1998. Lipid metabolism during exercise. *Sports Medicine* 26(1): 29–42.

Rodgers, C. D. 1998. Fuel metabolism during exercise: the role of the glucose–fatty acid cycle in mediating carbohydrate and fat metabolism. *Canadian Journal of Applied Physiology* 23(6): 528–533.

Roy, H. J., et al. 1998. Substrate oxidation and energy expenditure in athletes and nonathletes consuming isoenergetic high- and low-fat diets. *American Journal of Clinical Nutrition* 67: 405–411.

Saris, W. H. M., et al. 1989. Study on food intake and energy expenditure during extreme sustained exercise: the Tour de France. *International Journal of Sports Medicine* 10: S26–S31.

Satabin, P., et al. 1987. Metabolic and hormonal responses to lipid and carbohydrate diets during exercise in man. *Medicine and Science in Sports and Exercise* 19(3): 218–223.

Sherman, W. M. 1992. Recovery from endurance exercise. *Medicine and Science in Sports and Exercise* 24(9): S336–S339.

Sherman, W. M., and G. S. Wimer. 1991. Insufficient dietary carbohydrate during training: does it impair performance? *International Journal of Sport Nutrition* 1: 28–44.

Stainsby, W. N. 1986. Biochemical and physiological bases for lactate production. *Medicine and Science in Sports and Exercise* 18(3): 341–343.

Tarnopolsky, M. A., J. D. MacDougall, and S. A. Atkinson. 1988. Influence of protein intake and training status on nitrogen balance and lean body mass. *Journal of Applied Physiology* 64(1): 187–193.

Van Hall, G., S. M. Shirreffs, and J. A. L. Calbet. 2000. Muscle glycogen resynthesis during recovery from cycle exercise: no effect of additional protein ingestion. *Journal of Applied Physiology* 88: 1631–1636.

Whitley, H. A., et al. 1998. Metabolic and performance responses during endurance exercise after high-fat and high-carbohydrate meals. *Journal of Applied Physiology* 85(2): 418–424.

Williams, S. R. 1985. *Nutrition and Diet Therapy*, 5th ed. St. Louis: Times Mirror/Mosby.

Wright, D. A., W. M. Sherman, and A. R. Dernbach. 1991. Carbohydrate feedings before, during, or in combination improve cycling endurance performance. *Journal of Applied Physiology* 71(3): 1082–1088.

Zawadzki, K. M., B. B. Yaspelkis III, and J. L. Ivy. 1992. Carbohydrate-protein complex increases the rate of muscle glycogen storage after exercise. *Journal of Applied Physiology* 72(5): 1854–1859.

Chapter 3

Balaban, E. P., et al. 1995. The effect of running on serum and red cell ferritin. *International Journal of Sports Medicine* 16(5): 278–282.

Blick, R. L. 1993. *Hematology: Clinical and Laboratory Practice*, Vol. 1. St. Louis: Mosby.

Chatard, J. C., et al. 1999. Anaemia and iron deficiency in athletes. *Sports Medicine* 27(4): 229–240.

Eichner, E. R. 1992. Sports anemia, iron supplements, and blood doping. *Medicine and Science in Sports and Exercise* 24(9): S315–S318.

Friedmann, B., et al. 1999. Effects of iron supplementation on total body hemoglobin during endurance training at moderate altitude. *International Journal of Sports Medicine* 20: 78–85.

Nielsen, P., and D. Nachtigall. 1998. Iron supplementation in athletes. *Sports Medicine* 26(4): 207–216.

Snyder, A. C., et al. 1994. A simplified approach to estimating the maximal lactate steady state. *International Journal of Sports Medicine* 15(1): 27–31.

Van Handel, P. J. *What's in your Blood*. Internal Document: United States Olympic Committee, Sport Science and Coaching Department.

Chapters 6–10

Abernathy, P. J., R. Thayer, and A. W. Taylor. 1990. Acute and chronic responses of skeletal muscle to endurance and sprint training. *Sports Medicine* 10(6): 365–389.

Anderson, M. E., et al. 2000. Improved 2000-meter rowing performance in competitive oarswomen after caffeine ingestion. *International Journal of Sport Nutrition and Exercise Metabolism* 10: 446–476.

Applegate, E. 1999. Effective nutritional ergogenic aids. *International Journal of Sport Nutrition* 9: 229–239.

Bahrke, M. S., and W. P. Morgan. 1994. Evaluation of the ergogenic properties of ginseng. *Sports Medicine* 18(4): 229–248.

Bailey, D. M., et al. 1998. Implications of moderate altitude training for sea level endurance in elite distance runners. *European Journal of Applied Physiology* 78: 360–368.

Balsom, P. D., K. Söderlund, and B. Ekblom. 1994. Creatine in humans with special reference to creatine supplementation. *Sports Medicine* 18(4): 266–280.

Beckers, E. J., et al. 1992. Gastric emptying of carbohydrate–medium chained triglyceride suspensions at rest. *International Journal of Sports Medicine* 13: 581–584.

Behm, D. G., and D. G. Sale. 1993. Velocity specificity of resistance training. *Sports Medicine* 15(6): 374–388.

Bell, G. J., et al. 1993. Maintenance of strength gains while performing endurance training in oarswomen. *Canadian Journal of Applied Physiology* 18(1): 104–115.

Berglund, B. 1992. High altitude training: aspects of heamatological adaptation. *Sports Medicine* 14(5): 289–303.

Berning, J. R. 1996. The role of medium-chained triglycerides in exercise. *International Journal of Sport Nutrition* 6: 121–133.

Bogdanis, G. C., et al. 2000. Effect of different carbohydrate drinks on whole body carbohydrate storage after exhaustive exercise. *Journal of Applied Physiology* 88: 1529–1536.

Boutellier, U., et al. 1990. Aerobic performance at altitude: effects of acclimatization and hematocrit with reference to training. *International Journal of Sports Medicine* 11: S21–S26.

Brass, E. P., et al. 1993. Carnitine delays rat skeletal muscle fatigue in vitro. *Journal of Applied Physiology* 75(4): 1595–1600.

Braun, B., et al. 1991. Effects of coenzyme Q_{10} supplement on exercise performance, VO_2 max, and lipid peroxidation in trained cyclists. *International Journal of Sport Nutrition* 1: 353–365.

Brooks, G. A. 1987. Amino acids and protein metabolism during exercise and recovery. *Medicine and Science in Sports and Exercise* 19(5): S150–S156.

Burke, E. R. 1999. *Optimal Muscle Recovery* (pp. 148–149). Garden City Park, NY: Avery Publishing Group.

Butterfield, G. 1996. Ergogenic aids: evaluating sports nutrition products. *International Journal of Sport Nutrition* 6: 191–197.

Chambers, R. L, and J. C. McDermott. 1996. Molecular basis of skeletal muscle regeneration. *Canadian Journal of Applied Physiology* 21(3): 155–184.

Clarkson, P. M. 1996. Nutrition for improved sports performance. *Sports Medicine* 21(6): 393–401.

Clarkson, P. M., and I. Tremblay. 1988. Exercise-induced muscle damage, repair, and adaptation in humans. *Journal of Applied Physiology* 65(1): 1–6.

Cheuvront, S. N., et al. 1999. Effects of ENDUROX on metabolic responses to submaximal exercise. *International Journal of Sport Nutrition* 9: 434–442.

Coggan, A. R., and S. C. Swanson. 1992. Nutritional manipulations before and during endurance exercise: effects on performance. *Medicine and Science in Sports and Exercise* 24(9): S331–S335.

Conlee, R. 1991. Amphetamine, caffeine, and cocaine. In Lamb, D. L., and M. H. Williams (Eds.), *Perspectives in Exercise Science and Sports Medicine*, Vol. 4: *Ergonomics—Enhancement of Performance in Exercise and Sport* (p. 327). Ann Arbor, MI: Brown & Benchmark.

Cooper, D. M. 1994. Evidence for and mechanisms of exercise modulation of growth—an overview. *Medicine and Science in Sports and Exercise* 26(6): 733–740.

Costill, D. L., G. P. Dalsky, and W. J. Fink. 1978. Effects of caffeine ingestion on metabolism and exercise performance. *Medicine and Science in Sports and Exercise* 10(3): 155–158.

Coyle, E. F., et al. 1984. Time course of loss of adaptations after stopping prolonged intense endurance training. *Journal of Applied Physiology* 57(6): 1857–1864.

Davis, J. M., et al. 1999. Effects of branched-chain amino acids and carbohydrate on fatigue during intermittent, high-intensity running. *International Journal of Sports Medicine* 20: 309–314.

Davis, J. M., R. S. Welsh, and N. A. Alderson. 2000. Effects of carbohydrate and chromium ingestion during intermittent high-intensity exercise to fatigue. *International Journal of Sport Nutrition and Exercise Metabolism* 10: 476–485.

Decombaz, J., et al. 1983. Energy metabolism of medium-chain triglycerides versus carbohydrates during exercise. *European Journal of Applied Physiology* 52: 9–14.

Decombaz, J., et al. 1992. Muscle carnitine after strenuous endurance exercise. *Journal of Applied Physiology* 72(2): 423–427.

Decombaz, J., et al. 1993. Effects of L-carnitine on submaximal exercise metabolism after depletion of muscle glycogen. *Medicine and Science in Sports and Exercise* 25(6): 733–740.

Dick, F. W. 1992. Training at altitude in practice. *International Journal of Sports Medicine* 13: S203–S205.

Dodd, S. L., R. A. Herb, and S. K. Powers. 1993. Caffeine and exercise performance. *Sports Medicine* 15: 14–23.

Esbjörnsson-Liljedahl, M., et al. 1999. Metabolic response in type I and type II muscle fibers during a 30-s cycle spring in men and women. *Journal of Applied Physiology* 87(4): 1326–1332.

Eschbach, L. C., et al. 2000. The effect of Siberian ginseng on substrate utilization and performance during prolonged cycling. *International Journal of Sport Nutrition and Exercise Metabolism* 10: 444–451.

Essig, D., D. L. Costill, and P. J. Van Handel. 1980. Effects of caffeine ingestion on utilization of muscle glycogen and lipid during leg ergometer cycling. *International Journal of Sports Medicine* 1: 86–90.

Falk, B., et al. 1989. The effect of caffeine ingestion on physical performance after prolonged exercise. *European Journal of Applied Physiology* 59: 168–173.

Farretti, G., et al. 1990. Oxygen transport system before and after exposure to chronic hypoxia. *International Journal of Sports Medicine* 11: S15–S20.

Fry, R. W., A. R. Morton, and D. Keast. 1992. Periodisation and the prevention of overtraining. *Canadian Journal of Applied Physiology* 17(3): 241–248.

Fry, R. W., A. R. Morton, and D. Keast. 1992. Periodisation of training stress: a review. *Canadian Journal of Applied Physiology* 17(3): 234–240.

Gleeson, M., R. J. Maughan, and P. L. Greenhaff. 1986. Comparison of the effects of pre-exercise feeding of glucose, glycerol and placebo on endurance and fuel homeostasis in man. *European Journal of Applied Physiology* 55: 645–653.

Gohil, K., et al. 1987. Effect of exercise training on tissue vitamin E and ubiquinone content. *Journal of Applied Physiology* 63(4): 1638–1641.

Goldberg, A. L., et al. 1975. Mechanism of work-induced hypertrophy of skeletal muscle. *Medicine and Science in Sports and Exercise* 7(3): 185–198.

Graham, T. E., and L. L. Spriet. 1991. Performance and metabolic responses to a high caffeine dose during prolonged exercise. *Journal of Applied Physiology* 71(6): 2292–2298.

Green, H. J., et al. 1992. Altitude acclimatization and energy metabolic adaptations in skeletal muscle during exercise. *Journal of Applied Physiology* 73(6): 2701–2708.

Greer, F., C. McLean, and T. E. Graham. 1998. Caffeine, performance and metabolism during repeated Wingate exercise tests. *Journal of Applied Physiology* 85(4): 1502–1508.

Greig, C., et al. 1987. The effect of oral supplementation with L-carnitine on maximum and submaximum exercise capacity. *European Journal of Applied Physiology* 56: 457–460.

Gunga, H. C., et al. 1994. Time course of erythropoietin, triiodothyronine, thyroxine and thyroid-stimulating hormone at 2,315 m. *Journal of Applied Physiology* 76(3): 1068–1072.

Hirakoba, K., A. Maruyama, and K. Misaka. 1993. Effect of acute sodium bicarbonate ingestion on excess CO_2 output during incremental exercise. *European Journal of Applied Physiology* 66: 536–541.

Hitchins, S., et al. 1999. Glycerol hyperhydration improves cycle time trial performance in hot humid conditions. *European Journal of Applied Physiology* 80: 494–501.

Horswill, C. A. 1995. Effects of bicarbonate, citrate, and phosphate loading on performance. *International Journal of Sport Nutrition* 4: S111–S119.

Horswill, C. A., et al. 1988. Influence of sodium bicarbonate on sprint performance: relationship to dosage. *Medicine and Science in Sports and Exercise* 20(6): 566–569.

Houston, M. E. 1999. Gaining weight: the scientific basis of increasing skeletal muscle mass. *Canadian Journal of Applied Physiology* 24(4): 305–316.

Inder, W. J., et al. 1998. The effects of glycerol and desmopressin on exercise performance and hydration in triathletes. *Medicine and Science in Sports and Exercise* 30(8): 1263–1269.

Ivy, J. L., et al. 1979. Influence of caffeine and carbohydrate feedings on endurance performance. *Medicine and Science in Sports and Exercise* 11(1): 6–11.

Ivy, J. L., et al. 1988. Muscle glycogen synthesis after exercise: effect of time of carbohydrate ingestion. *Journal of Applied Physiology* 64(4): 1480–1485.

Jeukendrup, A. E., et al. 1996. Effects of endogenous carbohydrate availability on oral medium-chain triglyceride oxidation during prolonged exercise. *Journal of Applied Physiology* 80(3): 949–954.

Jeukendrup, A. E., et al. 1998. Effect of medium-chain triglycerol and carbohydrate ingestion during exercise on substrate utilization and subsequent cycling performance. *American Journal of Clinical Nutrition* 67: 397–404.

Jimenez, C., et al. 1999. Plasma volume changes during and after acute variations of body hydration level in humans. *European Journal of Applied Physiology* 80: 1–8.

Junderkrup, A. E., et al. 1992. Physiological changes in male competitive cyclists after two weeks of intensified training. *International Journal of Sports Medicine* 13(7): 534–541.

Katayama, K., et al. 2000. Cardiovascular response to hypoxia after endurance training at altitude and sea level and after detraining. *Journal of Applied Physiology* 88: 1221–1227.

Keith, S. P., I. Jacobs, and T. M. McLellan. 1992. Adaptations to training at the individual anaerobic threshold. *European Journal of Applied Physiology* 65: 316–323.

Keizer, H. A., et al. 1986. Influence of liquid and solid meals on muscle glycogen resynthesis, plasma fuel hormone response, and maximal physical working capacity. *International Journal of Sports Medicine* 8(2): 99–104.

Kenttä, G., and P. Hassmén. 1998. Overtraining and recovery. *Sports Medicine* 26(1): 1–16.

Knitter, A. E., et al. 2000. Effects of β-hydroxy-β-methylbutyrate on muscle damage after a prolonged run. *Journal of Applied Physiology* 89: 1340–1344.

Kreider, R. B. 1999. Dietary supplements and the promotion of muscle growth with resistance exercise. *Sports Medicine* 27(2): 97–110.

Kreider, R. B., et al. 1990. Effects of phosphate loading on oxygen uptake, ventilatory anaerobic threshold, and run performance. *Medicine and Science in Sports and Exercise* 22(2): 250–256.

Kreider, R. B., et al. 1992. Effects of phosphate loading on metabolic and myocardial responses to maximal and endurance exercise. *International Journal of Sport Nutrition* 2: 20–47.

Kreider, R. B., et al. 1999. Effects of calcium β-hydroxy-β-methylbutyrate (HMB) supplementation during resistance-training on markers of catabolism, body composition and strength. *International Journal of Sports Medicine* 20: 503–509.

Laaksonen, R., et al. 1995. Ubiquinone supplementation and exercise capacity in trained young and older men. *European Journal of Applied Physiology* 72: 95–100.

Lander, J. E., R. L. Simonton, and J. K. F. Giacobbe. 1990. The effectiveness of weight-belts during the squat exercise. *Medicine and Science in Sports and Exercise* 22(1): 117–126.

Lavender, G., and S. R. Bird. 1989. Effect of sodium bicarbonate ingestion upon repeated sprints. *British Journal of Sports Medicine* 23(1): 41–45.

Levine, B. D., et al. 1996. "Living high–training low": the effect of altitude acclimatization/normoxic training in trained runners. *Medicine and Science in Sports and Exercise* 23(4): S145.

Levine, B. D., and J. Stray-Gundersen. 1997. "Living high–training low": effect of moderate altitude acclimatization with low-altitude training on performance. *Journal of Applied Physiology* 83(1): 102–112.

Levine, B. D., and J. Stray-Gundersen. 1998. Altitude training does not improve running performance more than equivalent training near sea level in trained runners. *Medicine and Science in Sports and Exercise* 24(5): S596.

Londeree, B. R., and S. A. Ames. 1975. Maximal steady state versus state of conditioning. *European Journal of Applied Physiology* 34: 269–278.

Lucia, A., et al. 1998. Physiological differences between professional and elite road cyclists. *International Journal of Sports Medicine* 19: 342–348.

Lyons, T. P., et al. 1990. Effects of glycerol-induced hyperhydration prior to exercise in the heat on sweating and core temperature. *Medicine and Science in Sports and Exercise* 22(4): 477–483.

MacCartney, N., G. J. F. Heigenhauser, and N. L. Jones. 1983. Effects of pH on maximal power output and fatigue during short-term dynamic exercise. *Journal of Applied Physiology* 55(1): 225–229.

Mairbäurl, H. 1994. Red blood cell function in hypoxia at high altitude and exercise. *International Journal of Sports Medicine* 15: 51–63.

Mairbäurl, H., O. Oelz, and P. Bärtsch. 1993. Interactions between Hb, Mg, DPG, and Cl determine the change in Hb-oxygen affinity at high altitudes. *Journal of Applied Physiology* 74(1): 40–48.

Malm, C., et al. 1996. Supplementation with ubiquinone-10 causes cellular damage during intense exercise. *Acta Physiologica Scandinavica* 157: 511–512.

Malm, C., et al. 1997. Effects on ubiquinone-10 supplementation and high intensity training on physical performance in humans. *Acta Physiologica Scandinavica* 161: 379–384.

Martin, D. T. 1994. Stress hormones following intense cycling exercise: insights into overtraining. Unpublished doctoral dissertation. University of Wyoming, Laramie, WY.

Martin, D. T., et al. 1994. Effects of interval training and taper on cycling performance and isokinetic leg strength. *International Journal of Sports Medicine* 15: 485–491.

Massicotte, D., et al. 1992. Oxidation of exogenous medium-chain free fatty acids during prolonged exercise: comparison with glucose. *Journal of Applied Physiology* 73(4): 1334–1339.

Matson, L. G., and V. T. Zung. 1993. Effects of sodium bicarbonate ingestion on anaerobic performance: a meta-analytic review. *International Journal of Sport Nutrition* 3: 2–28.

Maughin, R. J., J. B. Leiper, and S. M. Shirreffs. 1996. Rehydration and recovery after exercise. *Sports Science Exchange* 9(3).

Mero, A. 1999. Leucine supplementation and intensive training. *Sports Medicine* 27(6): 347–358.

Miller, J. M., et al. 1983. Effect of glycerol feeding on endurance and metabolism during prolonged exercise in man. *Medicine and Science in Sports and Exercise* 15(3): 237–242.

Mittleman, K. D., M. R. Ricci, and S. P. Bailey. 1998. Branched-chain amino acids prolong exercise during heat stress in men and women. *Medicine and Science in Sports and Exercise* 30(1): 83–91.

Monteleone, P., et al. 1990. Effects of phosphatidylserine on the neuroendocrine response to physical stress in humans. *Neuroendocrinology* 52: 243–248.

Montner, P., et al. 1996. Pre-exercise glycerol hydration improves cycling endurance time. *International Journal of Sports Medicine* 17(1): 27–33.

Morris, D. M., et al. 2000. The effects of breathing supplemental oxygen during altitude training on cycling performance. *Journal of Science and Medicine in Sports* 3(2): 165–175.

Morrissey, M. C., E. A. Harman, and M. J. Johnson. 1995. Resistance training modes: specificity and effectiveness. *Medicine and Science in Sports and Exercise* 27(5): 648–660.

Murray, R., et al. 1991. Physiological responses to glycerol ingestion during exercise. *Journal of Applied Physiology* 71(1): 144–149.

Nissen, S., et al. 1996. Effect of leucine metabolite β-hydroxy-β-methylbutyrate on muscle metabolism during resistance-exercise training. *Journal of Applied Physiology* 81(5): 2095–2104.

Plowman, S. A., et al. 1999. The effects of ENDUROX on the physiological responses to stair-stepping exercise. *Research Quarterly for Exercise and Sport* 70(4): 385–388.

Poerter, D. A., et al. 1995. The effect of oral coenzyme Q_{10} on the exercise tolerance of middle-aged, untrained men. *International Journal of Sports Medicine* 16(7): 421–427.

Robergs, R., and S. E. Griffin. 1998. Glycerol: biochemistry, pharmacokinetics and clinical and practical applications. *Sports Medicine* 26(3): 145–167.

Sale, D. G. 1988. Neural adaptation to resistance training. *Medicine and Science in Sports and Exercise* 20(5): S135–S145.

Sands, W. A. 1992. Periodization and planning of training. *American Ski Coach,* Fall: 9–17.

Sasaki, H., I. Takaoka, and T. Ishiko. 1987. Effects of sucrose or caffeine ingestion on running performance and biochemical responses to endurance running. *International Journal of Sports Medicine* 8: 203–207.

Sasaki, H., et al. 1987. Effect of sucrose and caffeine ingestion on performance of prolonged strenuous running. *International Journal of Sports Medicine* 8: 261–265.

Schmidt, W., et al. 1993. Effects of chronic hypoxia and exercise on plasma erythropoietin in high-altitude residents. *Journal of Applied Physiology* 74(4): 1874–1878.

Serebrovskaya, T., and A. Ivashkevich. 1992. Effects of a 1-yr stay at altitude on ventilation, metabolism, and work capacity. *Journal of Applied Physiology* 73(5): 1749–1755.

Sherman, W. M. 1992. Recovery from endurance exercise. *Medicine and Science in Sports and Exercise* 24(9): S336–S339.

Sherman, W. M., and G. S. Wimer. 1991. Insufficient dietary carbohydrate during training: does it impair performance? *International Journal of Sport Nutrition* 1: 28–44.

Sherman, W. M., et al. 1993. Dietary carbohydrate, muscle glycogen, and exercise performance during 7 d of training. *American Journal of Clinical Nutrition* 57: 27–31.

Slater, G. J., and D. Jenkins. 2000. β-hydroxy-β-methylbutyrate (HMB) supplementation and the promotion of muscle growth and strength. *Sports Medicine* 30(2): 105–116.

Soop, M., et al. 1988. Influence of carnitine supplementation on muscle substrate and carnitine metabolism during exercise. *Journal of Applied Physiology* 64(6): 2394–2399.

Spreit, L. L., et al. 1992. Caffeine ingestion and muscle metabolism during prolonged exercise in humans. *American Journal of Physiology* 262: E891–E898.

Starkey, D. B., et al. 1996. Effect of resistance training on strength and muscle thickness. *Medicine and Science in Sports and Exercise* 28(10): 1311–1320.

Svensson, M., et al. 1999. Effect of Q_{10} supplementation on tissue Q_{10} levels and adenine nucleotide catabolism during high-intensity exercise. *International Journal of Sport Nutrition* 9: 166–180.

Tanaka, H., and T. Swensen. 1998. Impact of resistance training on endurance performance. *Sports Medicine* 25(3): 191–200.

Tarnopolsky, M. A. 1994. Caffeine and endurance performance. *Sports Medicine* 18(2): 109–125.

Tarnopolsky, M. A., et al. 1997. Postexercise protein-carbohydrate and carbohydrate supplements increase muscle glycogen in men and women. *Journal of Applied Physiology* 83(6): 1877–1883.

Taylor, A. W., and L. Bachman. 1999. The effects of endurance training on muscle fiber types and enzyme activities. *Canadian Journal of Applied Physiology* 24(1): 41–53.

Terrados, N., et al. 1990. Is hypoxia a stimulus for synthesis of oxidative enzymes and myoglobin? *Journal of Applied Physiology* 66(6): 2369–2372.

Trappe, S. W., et al. 1994. The effects of L-carnitine supplementation on performance during interval swimming. *International Journal of Sports Medicine* 15(4): 181–185.

Tremblay, M. S., S. D. Galloway, and J. R. Sexsmith. 1994. Ergogenic effects of phosphate loading: physiological fact or methodological fiction? *Canadian Journal of Applied Physiology* 19(1): 1–11.

van der Merwe, P. J., H. G. Luus, and J. G. Barnard. 1992. Caffeine in sport: influences of endurance exercise on the urinary caffeine concentration. *International Journal of Sports Medicine* 13: 74–76.

Van Zyl, C. G., et al. 1996. Effects of medium-chain triglyceride ingestion on fuel metabolism and cycling performance. *Journal of Applied Physiology* 80(6): 2217–2225.

Vukovich, M. D., D. L. Costill, and W. J. Fink. 1994. Carnitine supplementation: effect on muscle carnitine and glycogen content during exercise. *Medicine and Science in Sports and Exercise* 26(9): 1122–1129.

Weir, J., et al. 1987. A high carbohydrate diet negates the metabolic effects of caffeine during exercise. *Medicine and Science in Sports and Exercise* 19(2): 100–105.

Welch, H. G. 1987. Effects of hypoxia and hyperoxia on human performance. *Exercise and Sports Science Review* 15: 191–220.

Weston, S. B., et al. 1997. Does exogenous coenzyme Q_{10} affect aerobic capacity in endurance athletes? *International Journal of Sport Nutrition* 7: 197–206.

Wilber, R. L., et al. 2002. Effect of F_IO_2 on physiological responses and power output in trained cyclists at moderate altitude. *Medicine and Science in Sports and Exercise* 34(5): S1509.

Wilson, G. D., and H. G. Welch. 1975. Effects of hyperoxic gas mixtures on exercise tolerance in man. *Medicine and Science in Sports and Exercise* 7: 46–52.

Wolfel, E. E., et al. 1991. Oxygen transport during steady-state submaximal exercise in chronic hypoxia. *Journal of Applied Physiology* 70(3): 1129–1136.

Wright, D. A., W. M. Sherman, and A. R. Dernbach. 1991. Carbohydrate feedings before, during, or in combination improve cycling endurance performance. *Journal of Applied Physiology* 71(3): 1082–1088.

Zawadzki, K. M., B. B. Yaspelkis III, and J. L. Ivy. 1992. Carbohydrate-protein complex increases the rate of muscle glycogen storage after exercise. *Journal of Applied Physiology* 72(5): 1854–1859.

Index

About the Author

David Morris began racing bicycles at eighteen and began his studies of exercise physiology at the University of Missouri in 1986. After receiving a bachelor's degree in exercise physiology in 1989, he worked as the strength and conditioning coach at the U.S. Olympic Training Center in Lake Placid, New York. After a brief tenure with the U.S. Olympic Committee, Dave returned to the University of Missouri to pursue a master's degree in exercise physiology. While working on his graduate degree, he continued to race for the University of Missouri cycling team.

After receiving his master's degree in 1992, Dave worked as a sports physiologist at the U.S. Olympic Training Center in Colorado Springs. While at the USOTC, he worked extensively with USA Cycling on testing and evaluating elite cyclists and developing their training programs. In 1993, he left the U.S. Olympic Committee to pursue a doctorate in exercise physiology at Ohio State University.

After completing the coursework for his doctorate in December of 1994, Dave worked as a physiologist for USA Cycling's Project '96. Since leaving USA Cycling in December of 1996, he has run his own company focusing on cycling performance research, coaching, and consulting. By 2003, Dave's clients had won eighteen national championships, three World Cups, and two silver medals at the World Championships. He can be reached at www.racersready.com.